CROSSING THE RUBICON
SEVEN STEPS TO WRITING YOUR OWN PERSONAL STRATEGY

A practical, proven, system to bring clarity and focus to your personal and professional life

BY

JOHN BUTLER

© Copyright 2006 John Butler.
All rights reserved. No part of this publication may be reproduced, stored in a retrieval system, or transmitted, in any form or by any means, electronic, mechanical, photocopying, recording, or otherwise, without the written prior permission of the author.

Century Management
Century House, Newlands Business Park, Newlands Cross
Dublin 22, Ireland
Telephone: 0035314595950
Fax: 0035314595949
Email: johnbutler@centurymanagement.ie
Web:www.centurymanagement.ie

Note for Librarians: A cataloguing record for this book is available from Library and Archives Canada at www.collectionscanada.ca/amicus/index-e.html
ISBN 1-4120-9535-2

Printed in Victoria, BC, Canada. Printed on paper with minimum 30% recycled fibre.
Trafford's print shop runs on "green energy" from solar, wind and other environmentally-friendly power sources.

TRAFFORD
PUBLISHING

Offices in Canada, USA, Ireland and UK

Book sales for North America and international:
Trafford Publishing, 6E–2333 Government St.,
Victoria, BC V8T 4P4 CANADA
phone 250 383 6864 (toll-free 1 888 232 4444)
fax 250 383 6804; email to orders@trafford.com

Book sales in Europe:
Trafford Publishing (UK) Limited, 9 Park End Street, 2nd Floor
Oxford, UK OX1 1HH UNITED KINGDOM
phone 44 (0)1865 722 113 (local rate 0845 230 9701)
facsimile 44 (0)1865 722 868; info.uk@trafford.com

Order online at:
trafford.com/06-1290

10 9 8 7 6 5 4

DEDICATION

*To Imelda,
the most positive person on earth,
for inspiring me
and so many other individuals
to cross their own rubicon*

ACKNOWLEDGEMENTS

I have been very privileged to work with tens of thousands of great people who have 'taken the medicine' that I have been prescribing for almost 20 years and have *crossed the rubicon* of their own personal, professional and business lives.

These men and women, from all walks of life and nationalities, proved to me that you can make great things happen with determination and a disciplined approach.

Thank you for teaching me how to put the many metaphors that explain the rubicon phenomena into this book. The metaphor is understood by different people in different ways with concepts such as raising the bar to new heights, pushing out the boundaries of possibility, going from good to great, reaching the tipping point, time to get serious, breaking through the glass ceiling, becoming unstoppable, and more.

In a nutshell, this book "*Crossing the Rubicon*" is a metaphor, and a mechanism, for releasing your potential, transforming your life and achieving personal and professional success.

Appreciation also goes to Imelda, my business and life partner for giving me appropriate feedback during the draft stages. Michelle and Maria energise me with their enthusiasm for 'living life' and their clarity of purpose for the future. Thanks for the encouragement and the 'push' you give me.

Special acknowledgement goes to my PA, Suzanne Greene for her dedication and relentless persistence in making this happen. Suzanne knows every word, paragraph and chapter as well as I know it. Margaret Fogarty played a vital team role in bringing the project home.

TABLE OF CONTENTS

INTRODUCTION **11**
BACKGROUND AND PURPOSE **12**
WHAT DOES THE METAPHOR *CROSSING THE RUBICON* MEAN? **13**
WHAT IS STRATEGY? **14**
WHAT IS PERSONAL STRATEGY? **17**
WHY WRITE A PERSONAL STRATEGY? **20**
ARE YOU READY TO WRITE YOUR PERSONAL STRATEGY? **23**
WHAT ARE THE SEVEN STEPS IN THE RUBICON MODEL? **24**

RUBICON STEP 1: CURRENT SITUATION ANALYSIS ... THE NOW **26**
1.1 THE SUCCESS INDEX ... WHAT IS LIFE ALL ABOUT? **27**
    i. To Be Happy And Have Peace Of Mind 27
    ii. To Have Good Physical Health 29
    iii. To Be Committed To Quality Relationships 31
    iv. To Be Engaged In Purposeful Work 32
    v. To Have Financial Freedom 34
    vi. Self Actualisation: To Be Living A Full Life 35
1.2 SCRIPTING THE CURRENT STATUS ...WHAT IS YOUR OWN STORY? **38**
1.3 WHAT 'BUSINESS' ARE YOU IN? ... WHAT BUSINESS SHOULD YOU BE IN? **40**
1.4 SIX RESOURCES ANALYSIS ... HOW RESOURCEFUL ARE YOU? **43**
    i. The Money Resource 45
    ii. The Product Resource 46
    iii. The Physical Resource 47
    iv. The Intangible Resource 49
    v. The Time Resource 52
    vi. The People Resource 54
1.5 STRATEGIES FOR FINANCIAL INDEPENDENCE ... HOW DO YOU BECOME WEALTHY? **56**
    i. Four Categories Of Income Generation 56
    ii. How To Get The Luck Factor With Money 57
    iii. Three Levels Of Wealth 60
    iv. Five Pathways To Becoming Wealthy 63
    v. Five Value Drivers To Creating Wealth 65
1.6 TIME AND LIFE MANAGEMENT ... HOW DO YOU USE TIME? **74**
    i. Are You Being Reactive Or Proactive? 74
    ii. Are You Efficient Or Effective? 75
    iii. Do You Concentrate On Urgent Tasks Or Important Tasks? 76
    iv. What Is The Most Valuable Use Of Your Time Right Now? 77
    v. What Are You Doing Today To Achieve Your Long-Term Strategy? 78
    vi. What Makes You Productive? 79
    vii. What Can You, And Only You, Do? 79
    viii. What Would You Do Differently? 80

1.7 MASTERING THE CHALLENGES OF CHANGE ... WHAT CHOICES HAVE YOU? 81
    i. Transformational Change: Wide Scope, High Impact 81
    ii. Procedural Change: High Impact, Narrow Scope 83
    iii. Routine Change: Narrow Scope, Low Impact 83
    iv. Continuous Improvement: Low Impact, Wide Scope 83

1.8 TALENT ANALYSIS ... HOW DO YOU TURN YOUR TALENTS INTO COMPETENCIES? 85

1.9 PRODUCT/MARKET OVERVIEW ... DO YOU HAVE OPTIONS? 91
    i. Personal Market Penetration: Current Market, Current Product 92
    ii. Market Development: Current Product, New Market 92
    iii. Career Diversification: New Market, New Product 93
    iv. Professional Development: New Product, Current Market 94

1.10 SWOT ANALYSIS ... HOW DO YOU BUILD ON STRENGTHS AND MANAGE WEAKNESSES? 95
    i. Talents And Competencies 96
    ii. Skills Inventory 96
    iii. Processes, Functions, Roles. 96
    iv. Knowledge Management 96
    v. Creativity and Innovation 97
    vi. Physical Resources 97
    vii. Personal Identity And Image 97
    viii. Quality Control 98
    ix. Production 98
    x. Identification Of Critical Success Factors (CSFs) 98
    xi. Identification Of Choke Points 98

1.11 EMERGING PRIORITIES FROM CURRENT SITUATION ANALYSIS 100

RUBICON STEP 2: REVIEWING YOUR HISTORY ... THE PAST 101
    Five Areas to Explore 103
    i. Early Influences 103
    ii. School Years 103
    iii. Present Family Life 103
    iv. Health, Hobbies and Social Life 104
    v. Job and Career Assessment 104
    Stacking Up The Evidence 105
    i. Emotional Maturity 105
    ii. Achievement Orientation 106
    iii. Authority Conflict 106
    iv. Mental Stability 107
    v. Self-Image 107
    vi. Hardiness Test 107
    vii. Locus Of Control 108
    viii. Personal Values 108
    In Reviewing Your History 108

RUBICON STEP 3: CLARIFYING & ORDERING VALUES ... THE WHY 112
    How Do You Write A Set Of Values? 114

RUBICON STEP 4: CRYSTALLISING YOUR MISSION ... THE WHAT 118

RUBICON STEP 5: COMMITTING TO A CLEAR VISION ... THE FUTURE 122

The Behaviours Of The Great Visionaries 124
    i. How Do You Entertain Your Dreams? 125
    ii. Are You Building On Your Talents? 125
    iii. Do You Take 100 percent Responsibility For Your Life? 125
    iv. Why Haven't You Achieved This Vision Already? 126
    v. Are You Prepared To Work Hard Over Time? 126
    vi. What Words Sum Up Your Personal Brand? 126
    vii. How Much Discipline Have You? 127
    viii. How Decisive Are You? 127
    ix. How Good Are You At Service? 127
    x. Are You A Learner? 128

Examples of Vision Statements 128

Critical Success Factors Of The Vision Statement 129

RUBICON STEP 6: WRITING CLEAR STRATEGIC GOALS ... THE HOW 134

Best Practice Goal Setting 134
    i. Harmonious And Consistent Goals 134
    ii. Synchronise Your Talents With Your Goals 135
    iii. Hard Work, Luck, Opportunity And Goal Achieving 135
    iv. Variety Is The Spice Of Goal Setting 135

Clarity And Focus Regarding Strategy And Goal Setting 136
    Examples of Strategic Goals 138

RUBICON STEP 7: TACTICAL PLANNING & IMPLEMENTATION ... THE WHEN 142

THE FINAL CHECK 145
    i. Definition of 'The Principle Of The Objective' 147
    ii. Definition of 'The Principle Of The Offensive' 149
    iii. Definition of 'The Principle Of Mass' 151
    iv. Definition of 'The Principle Of Manoeuvre' 153
    v. Definition of 'The Principle Of Economy' 155
    vi. Definition of 'The Principle Of Exploitation' 157
    vii. Definition of 'The Principle Of Execution' 159
    viii. Definition of 'The Principle Of Surprise' 161

Beyond Strategy Formulation To Strategy Execution: Meet The Enemy 163
    i. Monitor The Execution.. 165

    ii. Monitor The Timeframes 166

EPILOGUE 167

APPENDICES 169
Appendix 1: Ireland: Crossing The Rubicon As A Country... 170

Appendix 2: Frequently Asked Questions 172

Appendix 3: Words From The Wise: The Challenges Of Crossing The Rubicon................... 177

Appendix 4: Carry On.. 180

Appendix 5: Promise Yourself.. 181

Appendix 6: About Century Management 182

Appendix 7: About John Butler,... 183

Appendix 8: Odyssey: The Business Of Consulting 185

INDEX 187

INTRODUCTION

BACKGROUND AND PURPOSE

Thank you for reading this book. In the pages ahead, you will find a systematic, practical and proven methodology to help you chart a clear course for your future direction.

I have been using the 'Rubicon Model' in business situations for almost 20 years with all kinds of organisations – from small and medium family enterprises to national and international corporations, and from education institutes to hospitals and sports teams.

Management consultants have been using this model throughout the world with business organisations and individual managers to great effect as outlined in my book *Successful Entrepreneurial Management: How to Create Personal and Business Advantage*.

Now, I have fine-tuned the formula from the original business model to be more suitable to your personal and professional situation in *Crossing the Rubicon: Seven Steps to Writing Your Own Personal Strategy*.

At the end of this book you will have:

- A general overview of strategy formulation and how it applies to your personal life and professional situation
- An explanation of the seven rubicon steps of strategic thinking and planning
- An overview of the eight powerful ingredients of all great personal and business strategies
- A step-by-step template to write up your personal strategy with detailed notes and suggestions to guide you
- A 'psychological compass' to keep you on track and guide you towards the execution of your strategy
- A blueprint to get feedback and suggestions from your coach, mentor or programme leader.

The corresponding workbook **Writing Your Personal Strategy: Formulating the Seven Strategy Steps From the Rubicon Model** is available in printed or electronic format where you can literally write your own book.

Live well, laugh often, leave a legacy!
John Butler

INTRODUCTION: What Does The Metaphor 'Crossing The Rubicon' Mean?

WHAT DOES THE METAPHOR *'CROSSING THE RUBICON'* MEAN?

The term *'crossing the rubicon'* goes back to Roman times. In 49 BC Julius Caesar crossed the rubicon river and entered Italy from Gaul with a standing army. To do so was treason, an act of audacity against the Roman state and it effectively started a bloody civil war.

Crossing the rubicon was the point of no return for Caesar. It was an act of war, an irreversible step with no turning back. He knew the implications of his actions. When he had crossed the river he declared "Jacta alea est" meaning "The die (or dice) is now cast, there is no going back, ever again". He was irrevocably committed to that course of action.

Crossing the rubicon is, therefore, a figure of speech for taking bold, decisive and irreversible action. It is the point of no return and a hugely symbolic statement. When you write your personal strategy you cross the point of no return in that you take control of your own life and set a transformational course of action into play.

When you *cross the rubicon* you effectively burn your bridges and face down your best excuses. You move from *knowing* about the steps to transform your situation to *doing* something very practical about it. 'To know and not to do is not yet to know' is how Confucius put it over 2500 years ago. Moving from knowing to doing is *crossing the rubicon*.

Crossing the rubicon is a metaphor for releasing your potential, transforming your life and achieving personal and professional success. It helps you make that move from *knowing* about the best ideas and success techniques to *doing* something practical about the implementation of your life's purpose.

Crossing the rubicon is a personal strategy exercise that provides you with a road map to pull all your thinking and ambitions together into one co-ordinated whole. It will enable you to link your personal motivators and character essentials with specific goals and action plans.

The central thrust of this book, therefore is to provide you with a mechanism to apply best practice business strategies to your personal and professional life. Knowing about the ingredients of success or competency management is not enough to realise your potential; you must integrate all the pieces of the jigsaw into your own special design.

CROSSING THE RUBICON: Seven Steps To Writing Your Own Personal Strategy

WHAT IS STRATEGY?

Strategy is about bringing clarity, focus and execution to what you already know about your current situation and unlocking the potential of your future direction. Military and business definitions are the basis on which we develop an understanding of strategy. So, what is strategy? Some interpretations are:

1. **Strategy Is A Plan:** At face value, strategy is a clearly defined way of dealing with a certain kind of situation. For example, a business has a strategy to launch a new product and dominate a market. A political party has a strategy to win an election and get into government to have its policies implemented. A sports team has a strategy on how to play a match or win a championship. A child has a strategy to organise a birthday party.

   According to this interpretation, strategy has two essential characteristics. It is made in advance of the actions to which it applies, and it is developed consciously and purposefully. The cause of much of the confusion and mystification about strategy is that in sport, in politics, in the military and in management, strategy has been interpreted as being just a plan of doing things. But it's much more than that, especially as it applies to your personal and professional world.

   The key to becoming an effective strategist is the realisation that strategy is much more than just planning. It's about formulation of the plan and how the whole is greater than the sum of the parts. Strategic planning is, ironically, relatively easy. It is strategic thinking that separates the amateurs from the professionals. Strategic development then becomes a personal leadership competency.

2. **Strategy Is A Way Of Thinking:** Strategic thinking is a mind-set that must be continuously worked at. *If you don't use it, you lose it.* Just as strategy in a business is everyone's job so it should be a core practice in your personal life. In fact, the cultures of some organisations have developed from the influence of one person, then spread to a core team, and eventually a whole organisation. Hewlett Packard have developed *The HP Way*. It started with two founders, Bill Hewlett and David Packard, working in a garage building

testing equipment. The consistency of the McDonald's product in 30,000 outlets world-wide is derived from its thinking about Q, S, C and V – *'Quality, Service, Cleanliness and Value'*.

Personal strategic thinking is about gaining an awareness of the bigger picture and thinking outside the box. It's finding insights into the here and now and aligning those insights with your long term perspective. Thinking about thinking is a prerequisite to formulating a good strategy. In your day to day life you may say and think a lot of things but establishing the truth in your words and thoughts seems to be an overarching aim for all humans.

The purpose of <u>strategic thinking</u> is to explore novel, imaginative ways to differentiate your personal and professional positioning. It's personal and professional brand formulation. <u>Strategic planning</u> is the process of putting operational wheels on the strategies emerging from this thinking process. The 'secret' success of business or personal strategy is to integrate strategic thinking and strategic planning into your overall process.

3. **Strategy Is A Manoeuvre:** A manager explained why he got promoted over four other colleagues: "Simple," he said "I came in early, stayed late and volunteered for every ugly project my boss had on his desk". In this sense, strategy can be used as a ploy or as a threat to out-wit rivals and gain a competitive edge. Finding the alternative or 'the third right answer' is the essence of manoeuvre. Are you flexible enough to adjust the plan to the conditions as they emerge? How good are you at anticipating optimum outcomes? Are you a learner? Have you a 'Plan B'?

Formulating a strategy is often unstructured until you finally set the strategy down in writing. However, while the strategy is definite you must be flexible in how you achieve it because unforeseen things happen that require you to be flexible and smart enough to find another way.

4. **Strategy Is A Sequence Of Actions:** Strategy is also about the pattern of activities that you might engage in to achieve your objectives. A friend's objective was to build a new house within one year. His sequence of actions was to save money for a mortgage deposit, identify and buy a site, get a

mortgage, work with the architect on design, appoint a reliable builder, subcontract as much as possible, move in, landscape the garden and complete the interior design.

Ultimately, everything gets done in bite size pieces. Understanding that good planning is 'back from the future' planning, not from today forward is the essence of strategy. The natural urge to take action and launch militates against the strategy ethos. Aligning today's work with the big objective is the aim.

5. **Strategy Is Positioning:** Business positioning is all about specialisation, differentiation, segmentation and concentration. Specialisation means you become expert in a particular area – servicing your customers for example. Differentiation means you establish and brand a unique selling proposition. Segmentation means sub-dividing or carving up the market for selling and marketing purposes. Concentration means single-minded application of effort to the position taken. Positioning is about creating advantage or the upper hand for yourself. Your position in the world has got to do with status, rank, standing, stature, prestige, influence and reputation with others. 'Taking a position' on a matter shows you think strategically, that you have underlying principles, viewpoints and opinions that are thought out.

The word strategy itself comes from the Greek word *strategos* which means the art or science of being a (military) General. So, at its most basic, strategy is concerned with the general or overall objective. The Greek and Roman Generals knew that wars were won by a careful 'general' management of politics, logistics, planning tactics and taking action and the parallels between military and business strategy can be made throughout all periods of history. At a lower level, the General must decide and carry out the tactics (which comes from another Greek word *taktikos* meaning 'fit for arranging') to be deployed especially during contact with the enemy. In the tactics to capture an important city, for example, the General may decide to lay siege to it or scale the walls. Day-to-day business affairs are like a series of battles in a war. Of course, if the overall strategy is correct a number of tactical errors can be made without hindering the achievement of the overall objectives, general outcome or master strategy.

WHAT IS PERSONAL STRATEGY?

Personal Strategy is beyond goal setting, career planning and personal coaching. It is personal leadership, talent management and motivational planning all rolled into one. It is about maximising your personal capital. It is about formulating a clarity, purpose and high degree of expectation to your current personal/professional situation and future direction. It builds a framework or set of tracks for your desired future.

Rubicon strategists seek to make enormous surges forward, to cross their own rubicon river, to leverage, to accelerate, to multiply and to use forced multipliers. A forced multiplier is an integrated force that gives you extra power to leverage a situation and dramatically change the odds in your favour. Developing quality relationships with key influencers because of a networking strategy is a good example of accelerating your efforts.

"Yes, but I'm already doing very well" explained one hard working executive, "why should I undertake a rubicon?" You may be a good citizen and get up each day and go to work. Just doing that, you may achieve lots of tasks and accomplishments, even get promoted and become wealthy. However, that is not strategic planning, that is tactical operational planning and is for people who are obsessed with to do lists, projects, tasks and short term goals.

The primary objective of writing a personal strategy is to help you transform your life for the better and achieve the goals you set – this is the key – for yourself, not just to achieve the goals that circumstances deliver. A compelling rubicon strategy is 'an integrated whole' rather than a 'bits and parts' approach to personal and professional management.

Personal strategy is a perspective builder, a focused way of helping you see your world in the best way possible. In this respect, it should relate to you on a personal level, the way that competency management does on a professional level, or return on investment does on a commercial level. It contains the sum of your grand strategy. It integrates your driving forces, passions, character traits and world-view.

Developing strategic thinking means developing an appreciation of your talents and turning them into superior competencies to help you get from where you are to where you want to go. Remember, the rubicon model applies specifically to the personal and professional strategic arena.

This model helps you gather, integrate and co-ordinate the physical, intellectual, emotional and even spiritual qualities you have as a person and as a professional. Many brilliant technical strategies fail because they fail to connect on all these four levels.

You are not just a professional with a job, you are a human being who plays out many life roles — who 'wears many hats' — and this process endeavours to scope all of these roles or 'hats'.

The rubicon personal strategy model translates perfectly to the family situation. You and your spouse/partner could take a long weekend in some quiet hotel or guest house and lock yourselves away to concentrate on building a joint family strategy, bringing the project to completion together. Peace and quiet, a deadline and a reward at the end will induce your creative juices towards providing joint solutions.

You would not build a sun-room in your back garden without thinking and planning it out on paper, why build your life without thinking and planning it out on paper also? One manifestation of this is that the financial affairs of the majority of men and women is poor to bad after a lifetime of toil and labour. In fact, most people end up broke or dependent.

Further, the second biggest disease by 2010 will be stress and depression according to the World Health Organisation. In many countries more than half the population are overweight with some 20 percent in the obese category. On these two considerations alone, you have every reason to write your personal strategy to differentiate yourself, to live a life full of promise and potential.

There are four personal leadership qualities that will be important for you to keep top of mind as you set about this project:

- **Realism:** Being realistic means seeing things as they really are, not as you would like them to be. The truth may hurt but make sure it is the truth. It means not avoiding or denying the real issues in your personal or professional life.

- **Responsibility:** Taking responsibility means having the courage to respond positively to life and work situations. It means not blaming other people or making excuses for your circumstances. It means setting a strategy 'to get on with it'.

- **Boldness:** Being bold means taking the actions necessary, despite your fears. The similarity between the coward and the courageous person is that both of them have fears but the difference is that the person with courage acts in spite of their fears while the coward fails to act. Winston Churchill once said "Courage is rightly considered the foremost of all the virtues because upon it, all other virtues depend".

- **Purpose:** Harnessing the power of purpose is the key to success. Have you a clear purpose? A significance? The challenge is to crystallise it and live it. Writing a personal strategy for the sake of strategy is not strategy. It's a clinical plan at best. Strategy with purpose needs to integrate your whole life so that the sum is always greater than the combination of its parts. Purpose is what, ultimately, separates humans from animals.

Crossing the rubicon is 'dangerous' in that it forces you out of the comfort zone of life and helps you burn some bridges, which prevents you from reverting to type or doing what comes easy. Personal leadership is best manifest by doing what great leaders do – they 'get real', they accept 100 percent responsibility, they take courage, and they live their lives on purpose.

Three bricklayers who worked side by side on a building site provide the classic story of the philosophy of personal strategy. A passer-by asked the first bricklayer what he was doing. He replied: 'I'm laying some bricks.' The passer-by asked the same question of the second bricklayer, who replied: 'I'm building a wall'. In reply to the same question, the third bricklayer said: 'I'm building a cathedral'. Putting all your initiatives into a total long-term solutions framework, not a short-term, quick fix framework is the essence of personal strategy. A cathedral is a far greater vision than a mere brick wall. Personal strategy is about putting the structures in place, brick by brick, wall by wall, to help you build the cathedral of life – your life.

WHY WRITE A PERSONAL STRATEGY?

Reasons are the fuel in the furnace of progress. Reasons energise. Reasons give clarity. Reasons motivate. Reasons give good cause. 'To reason something out' is to find a solution to a problem by considering possible options. You may not have written up your personal strategy to date because your reasons have been unclear. Do any of these four negative reasons – blockages – apply to you:

1. **Importance Not Emphasised:** You did not understand the importance of the personal strategy exercise to your long-term success. Neither at home, nor at school does the importance of writing a personal strategy get much attention. From now, you need to understand the context and significance of the exercise as a long-term investment in your life.

2. **Methodology Unclear:** Up to now, perhaps, you did not know how to craft a comprehensive strategy simply because you never understood the need to or found a methodology to do so. You can eliminate both of these reasons from now. The seven step rubicon methodology is all embracing. You now know the importance and have a methodology to hand.

3. **Commitment Lacking:** Writing your personal strategy takes a minimum of 30 hours from the time you start writing. Add another 30 hours (at least) to read your way into the subject and another 30 hours to tidy up and you will see why lack of commitment leads to hesitation and procrastination. You may not have been prepared to give the necessary time commitment up to now because you had no system to do it or were unclear about how to do it. Now, you can make ready with no 'hold back' excuses hanging around.

4. **Fear Stops You Starting:** Your failure and rejection subconscious inhibitors may have been prowling. Fear of failure is the single biggest inhibitor of human performance and living the good life. It paralyses initiative and sabotages progress. It's not that you cannot do things, it's that you have convinced yourself that you cannot do things. Fear is the

underlying reason – the good cause – why most things do not even get started. Be aware of this.

Being clear about what could be stopping you from doing this kind of project is the first step in releasing your breaks. The second step is to have absolute clarity around 'the positive reasons why' you should cross the rubicon. When the WHY is big enough – when the positive reasons are clear – the HOW is relatively simple.

Here are four excellent – positive – reasons to *cross the rubicon* and complete this Personal Strategy exercise:

1. **Personal Strategy Integrates And Respects The Need To Accommodate '*The Total You*':** Your many functional roles and responsibilities (e.g. parent, manager, son/daughter, professional, partner) need to be synchronised with your dreams, hopes, aspirations and inner calling. "To thine own self be true" as Shakespeare put it, remains the great challenge for everyone.

    Finding a compatibility between '*what you do*' and '*who you are*' is the goal. Rubicon will discipline you to look at your talents and how to best deploy them for maximum benefit and fulfilment. It will reveal opportunities available to you and reduce threats to your security and potential.

2. **Personal Strategy Enables You To Find Balance Between Your Home And Work Life:** When you bring a sense of balance to your work and home, both dimensions of your life benefit. Most people neglect, by omission, one area over the other. By giving attention to this balance you automatically feed your inner human needs and professional development. No amount of success and achievement in the professional domain will compensate for unhappiness in personal relationships and at home. Balance is the condition in which both dimensions of your life are equal or in correct proportions.

3. **Personal Strategy Helps Put The '*Nice To Know*' Ideas Into Action Plans:** The discipline of getting things done across all the dimensions of your life is vital to success. Confusion and stress emerge when one area is

neglected. Knowing about self-help methods and attending programmes breeds cynicism and scepticism if the missing link of execution is not adhered to across all the dimensions of your life.

So, rubicon becomes a framework to assess your plans and long-term decisions over time. The most exciting book you will ever read is the tome you write about yourself. And you will read it over and over again. But first, you must write it. The corresponding workbook *'Writing Your Personal Strategy: Formulating the Seven Strategy Steps From the Rubicon Model'* is that book.

4. **Personal Strategy Brings You To An Appreciation Of Tapping Into Your Talents And Values And How To Lead A Holistic, Principle-Based Approach To Life:** You will never be truly happy or achieve the degree of success you desire unless you find your true purpose. This exercise synchronises your personality and purpose with your actions like no other process. It brings focus and clarity to your energies, lifestyle, wealth creation and management potential.

It takes you beyond planning, beyond goals, beyond dreaming, to significance, to *'being'* all that you can be, to implementing your heart's desire, to raising the bar and to have that sense that you have lived, learned, loved and left a legacy that is worthy of your highest ideals and dreams.

The rubicon process is an integral part of talent management and is designed to turn your inborn and acquired talents into superior competencies to help you achieve this unique feat. Fear of failure and rejection are the great inhibitors of human potential. You need to understand fear in all its dimensions to master it. Most people have no idea that fear is the flip-side of 'the success secret'. This process is a master course in pushing out your boundaries of success and unlocking your full potential.

Writing your personal strategy will give you a discipline, a purpose and systems thinking to help you see patterns and areas for attention in your life. Unfortunately, we usually focus on isolated parts of the system and wonder why our efforts to solve problems and perpetuate success fail.

ARE YOU READY TO WRITE YOUR PERSONAL STRATEGY?

Your state of readiness to engage in the rubicon process is paramount to its success and this means giving consideration to two important dimensions.

First, you must get psychologically ready. This means having an open mind and the courage to explore this area of your development. The voices of cynicism and doubt will nudge at you right up to the starting point. These two imposters – self-doubt and cynicism – are mental defence mechanisms that only serve to sabotage you.

Second, you must learn the system. Readiness means having a general understanding of the strategy process – formulation, execution, strategic thinking and strategic planning. To formulate strategy you must understand the context and principles of strategy. Otherwise you work in a vacuum.

Readiness also means understanding that high levels of concentration are required. Intense concentration needs four essentials:

1. **Place:** Finding a place where you can be quiet. A table or desk at home is perfect. Finding a quiet corner at home can be easier said than done, but find it you must. This place becomes your 'zone' and if you work it properly, it becomes sacrosanct.

2. **Routine:** Establishing a routine also helps, such as early morning or the last couple of hours in the evening. Saturday morning 6-10 a.m. is an example. All great authors say this is the secret. Same time, same place, same routine. Get going, then follow the routine.

3. **Focus:** Minimising distractions can be as difficult at home as at work. You have to inform people of your intentions. Turn off everything – the TV, radio, mobile – to focus. Focus is one of the lost arts. Learn to focus for several hours at one time and you will conquer the world.

4. **Commitment:** Without commitment there is hesitation, the chance to draw back. This always leads to mediocrity and procrastination. And procrastination is the theft of time and life. Going from good to great is the magnificent obsession in the rubicon process. Commitment has to be worked at.

WHAT ARE THE SEVEN STEPS IN THE RUBICON MODEL?

When you are clear in your thinking about the ultimate reasons for setting a strategy and are prepared to give it the necessary time, you are then ready for the strategy formulation stage. The execution of a compelling, well formulated strategy is, of course, the second stage of all good strategy. But first comes strategy formulation, the biggest step and the primary focus of this book.

The rubicon model is a seven step system to enable you to formulate your strategy document and set about accomplishing your personal and professional objectives. The seven steps in the process are:

RUBICON STEP 1: CURRENT SITUATION ANALYSIS … THE NOW
RUBICON STEP 2: REVIEWING YOUR HISTORY … THE PAST
RUBICON STEP 3: CLARIFYING & ORDERING VALUES … THE WHY
RUBICON STEP 4: CRYSTALLISING YOUR MISSION … THE WHAT
RUBICON STEP 5: COMMITTING TO A CLEAR VISION … THE FUTURE
RUBICON STEP 6: WRITING CLEAR STRATEGIC GOALS … THE HOW
RUBICON STEP 7: TACTICAL PLANNING & IMPLEMENTATION … THE WHEN

Each step is explained in great detail in the following pages and more directional notes are given in the workbook, **Writing Your Personal Strategy: Formulating the Seven Strategy Steps From the Rubicon Model**. How do you proceed from here? Do you read all of this book first and then systematically start the writing process in the workbook? Or do you proceed step by step from here? The answer: Everything works. Follow your own preferred way … just do it.

Personal strategy formulation is a forced response exercise. It puts you on the spot to answer top of mind questions and in most cases what you write will be very accurate in your first attempt. Go with the flow. Just keep on writing.

'Forced response' writing helps you 'meet yourself' on the page. It crystallises your thinking into concrete form. It allows the 'chatter-box' in your mind to quieten while you script your multitudinous thoughts. There is a therapy in writing. And a power. Just trust the process. Start. Do it!

RUBICON STEP 1

Current Situation Analysis ... The Now

| RUBICON STEP 1 |
| CURRENT SITUATION ANALYSIS |

| RUBICON STEP 2 |
| REVIEWING YOUR HISTORY |

| RUBICON STEP 3 |
| CLARIFYING & ORDERING VALUES |

| RUBICON STEP 4 |
| CRYSTALLISING YOUR MISSION |

| RUBICON STEP 5 |
| COMMITTING TO A CLEAR VISION |

| RUBICON STEP 6 |
| WRITING CLEAR STRATEGIC GOALS |

| RUBICON STEP 7 |
| TACTICAL PLANNING & IMPLEMENTATION |

"Taking stock of the current state of affairs in your life is the starting point of personal and professional strategy"

RUBICON STEP 1: CURRENT SITUATION ANALYSIS ... THE NOW

Strategy formulation is the first vital step in strategy management and it always starts with 'taking stock' or a current situation analysis. Strategy execution is the second step in the strategy process and only becomes fully relevant when the formulation stage is completed.

Your current situation is a snapshot of how you see the current 'state of affairs' in your personal/home life and your professional/career life. It is a kind of 'balance sheet' and a reality check of your key success indicators at this point in time. More importantly, the seeds of future reality are close at hand in your current activities. The overall objective is to bring clarity to your current situation, before you can focus on the future. You can review eleven areas of your current situation as follows:

1.1 The Success Index ... What Is Life All About?
1.2 Scripting The Current Status ... What Is Your Own Story?
1.3 What 'Business' Are You In? ... What Business Should You Be In?
1.4 Six Resources Analysis ... How Resourceful Are You?
1.5 Strategies For Financial Independence ... How Do You Become Wealthy?
1.6 Time And Life Management ... How Do You Use Time?
1.7 Mastering The Challenges Of Change ... What Choices Have You?
1.8 Talent Analysis ... How Do You Turn Your Talents Into Competencies?
1.9 Product/Market Overview ... Do You Have Options?
1.10 Swot Analysis ... How Do You Build On Strengths And Manage Weaknesses?
1.11 Ten Emerging Priorities From Current Situation Analysis

The current situation analysis may appear to get a more comprehensive treatment in this book on first examination. Someone once said "If you can keep one eye on the past and one eye on the future you could go cross-eyed in the present". The current situation assessment is present tense and, if completed, sets the platform to dream and plan well into the future. Your past is good as a reference for learning, your future is where you will live, but your present is the benchmark for your strategy. A journey of a thousand miles starts with the first step. Assess 'the now' as your first step.

1.1 THE SUCCESS INDEX ... WHAT IS LIFE ALL ABOUT?

What is success? How successful are you, really? What criteria are you using to determine how you are doing? Maybe it is time to look at success again. Sometimes a fresh insight into success is worth a lifetime of experience.

You may have found some myths and much confusion about the concept of success. Success, however, leaves tracks. 'Total success' should embrace your full life, not one or two aspects of your endeavours. For example, many managers and business owners focus on the financial or achievement aspects over the more human factors of success. Here are six ingredients of success, ranked in order of importance, for you to consider:

i. TO BE HAPPY AND HAVE PEACE OF MIND

Peace of mind means to be in control of your own destiny. To be contented. To be enjoying the journey of life. To feel connected physically, mentally, emotionally and spiritually. To be carefree. To laugh. Just 'to be'. Less 'have' and 'do' and more 'be'. To be happy.

Happiness is the progressive realisation of a worthy goal. What is your worthy goal? What is your heart's desire? What motivates you? What do you believe in? These questions should prompt you to assess your values, which are at the very core of *who you are*, that is, your character.

The key to happiness is your determination to dedicate yourself to a worthwhile purpose by developing a certain mastery in your personal and professional competencies that are consistent with your natural talents, behaviours, values and intelligences. So, you can't be truly happy until you are clear about the inherent possibilities within your own personality. In other words, you are happy or unhappy to the degree you are in control of your life and know *who you are* and *what you do*.

The happiest people are those who have high levels of self-regard, self-confidence and personal pride. The good news is you can learn to be happy. Unfortunately many unhappy people don't know or accept this and fail to take responsibility for this anchor ingredient of success. You will be unlikely to get peace of mind and happiness by 'trying to be happy'. It seems to come as a result of doing day-to-day worthwhile work.

Paul Martin, a biologist with a PhD in behavioural biology, is the author of *Making Happy People – the nature of happiness and its origins in childhood*. In addition to trawling through the social psychology literature, he shares his own insights.

Martin defines happiness as a mental state composed of three elements. First, pleasure which is the emotional sensation of feeling good in the here and now. Second, the absence of displeasure which is freedom from anxiety and pain. Third is satisfaction with life in general or at least with aspects such as relationships, career or physical abilities. He also presents the argument for a fourth dimension of happiness, which is linked to having a deeper meaning or purpose in life. This dimension of happiness, both psychologists and philosophers agree, is often found through your religious beliefs.

So what makes some people happier than others and how can we help our children be happy? Martin suggests there are a number of aspects which contribute to a feeling of happiness. These include a connectedness to other people through personal relationships, a social and emotional competence (i.e. an ability to deal with your feelings and those of others so you can maintain those relationships), engagement in meaningful activity, a sense of control, optimism (as opposed to self-delusion) and outward focus.

Ireland, as a nation, scores very high on the *World Values Survey* with 77 percent of Irish people saying they are 'very proud' of their country. Forty two percent of Irish people are 'very happy' according to *The Economist* Intelligence Unit Research on Quality of Life Index.

Is happiness – as an individual, community, family, company – the greatest quality you can experience? Ironically, the great Irish playwright John B. Keane said that "Nobody in Ireland will be happy until everyone is better off than everyone else."

The evidence of unhappiness is encapsulated in the best kept secret of human life. This secret is fear. Fear manifests itself in a multitude of emotions such as self-doubt, poor self-image, shyness, guilt, blaming, anxiety, stress and mental distress/disorder. These emotions are learned behaviours that rob us of peace of mind and our natural right to be happy. Because the emotions associated with unhappiness are learned behaviours, they can be unlearned. Dale Carnegie once said "The person who seeks all their applause from outside has their happiness in another person's keeping".

You are where you are today on the happiness-unhappiness scale, largely because of *who you are* and the past choices you have made. The bottom line is you deserve to be happy and have peace of mind. You must, however, take 100 percent personal responsibility for learning how to do this. Trust your own best judgement now and give yourself a score in the personal strategy workbook. The best straw poll test of unhappiness is the levels of stress, anguish or frustration you experience.

ii. To Have Good Physical Health

Good physical health means being fit and energetic, to have vitality and a zest for living. It means eating well, exercising and resting enough to replenish the body.

Nature has a natural bias toward balance and harmony. Your body has a natural bias towards health and energy. Only improper treatment and incorrect operation cause it to get out of balance. Just as your inner voice will tell you if your peace of mind is off-track, so your body will let you know through lethargy, pain, illness and disease that it is out of alignment.

The Exhaust Epidemic was the headline for a feature article – Irish Times – on why up to 20 percent of people are 'running on empty' from a series of fatigue related illnesses including anaemia (unusual tiredness), chronic fatigue syndrome (overwhelming exhaustion), depression (loss of energy), type two diabetes (extreme tiredness), and sleep apnoea (daytime sleepiness).

Another piece of research *The Alameda Study* tracks the health habits of 8,000 men over 20 years to determine such factors as longevity, sickness patterns and why some men were healthier than others. The seven common habits of the healthiest ones were as follows: They eat at regular times each day, they eat lightly, especially fruit, vegetables and lean source protein, they do not graze between meals, they do not smoke, they have a moderate alcohol consumption, they are well rested with seven to eight hours sleep every night, and finally, they get regular exercise, which helps digestion and the overall 'feel good' factor.

World Health Organisation (WHO) guidelines suggest that obesity is rapidly reaching epidemic proportions with six out of 10 adults being overweight or obese. The 2005 *Irish National Task Force on Obesity* reports that 50 percent of men are overweight and 14 percent are obese. For women, the figures are 30 percent overweight and 12 percent obese.

Childhood obesity is growing exponentially all over the world. Ireland is one of five European countries – England, Cyprus, Sweden, Greece – that have reported overweight and obesity levels exceeding 20 percent among 7-11 year old children. There are more than 14 million overweight children in Europe. Jamie Oliver, the celebrity chef, says "This will be the first ever generation of children to die before their parents".

Diabetes is set to double over the next 10 years to 240 million worldwide. In Ireland, estimates are that 200,000 men and women have been diagnosed with diabetes with another 100,000 being unaware they have it. Diabetes is set to become the biggest killer of the 21st century. New York is the diabetes capital of the world with up to 15 percent of the population suffering from the disease. Diabetes is a condition where your body has trouble turning food into energy or glucose. Doctors place the blame on unhealthy diets and poor exercise. People with diabetes are up to four times more likely to suffer from heart disease, kidney damage and loss of eyesight.

Get to understand your weight from a medical perspective. Body Mass Index (BMI) measures body fat according to height and weight. If your BMI is below 20 you are considered underweight. A BMI score between 20-25 puts you in the normal category. If you score in the 30-35 range, you are class one obese and if you score in the 35-40 range you are class two obese. Class three obese is over a 40 BMI.

Counter arguments are emerging, suggesting that those kinds of figures are exaggerated and that the consequences of obesity are over played. Keeping all this in mind, there is no doubt that we need to 'eat less and exercise more' as a basic rule of vitality and physical wellbeing. How do you score on energy, vitality and good physical health?

iii. To Be Committed To Quality Relationships

The third ingredient of success is the quality of your relationships. Interpersonal intelligence has been defined as your ability to get along well with a wide range of other people such as your partner in life, your wider family, boss, teachers, colleagues and stakeholders of various kinds in your personal and business worlds. The calibre of your one-to-one relationships, above all, is a key determinant of your character and who you have become.

The quality of your life at home and at work is largely determined by your ongoing ability to communicate, negotiate, interact, persuade and influence other people. While most relationships are functional, that is, time and circumstance related, your ability to connect with and maintain, long-lasting friendship with 'the critical few' is vital to this success anchor. You are a 'work in progress', ever-growing and learning from the experiences of life. Your personality and character are shaped by how you learn to cope with the difference and uniqueness of other human beings more than any other factor.

Each person is unique and complex. Therefore, relationships are unique and complex and provide the arena to test one of the most fundamental success anchors. Following certain time-honoured truths or principles certainly helps. Here are four:

- **Trust:** Trust is the willingness to be vulnerable to another person's actions based on your experience that their actions have some importance to you. Trust means keeping your word and being consistent and dependable. Your most fundamental responsibility is that you are 'put in a position of trust' for your own life. Trust is the underlying rock of all personal and business relationships. Einstein said "Every kind of peaceful cooperation is based on mutual trust and only second on an institution such as a court of justice or the police". How much do you extend trust to those you interact with and how trustworthy are you?

- **Respect:** Respect primarily means listening attentively and giving due regard for the feelings and rights of others. When you 'show respect' to someone, you show a feeling of deep admiration which is elicited by their qualities and achievements. E. M. Forster, the English author, once wrote "I write to gain the respect of those I respect". We are driven to seek the respect of significant people in our lives. How respectful do you feel you are?

- **Openness:** Open communication requires time, helpfulness, attention and appreciation of the differences that another person brings to every one-to-one interaction. Openness means having the courage to reveal a little bit of your own vulnerable side. Self-revelation leads to a higher level of self-awareness. Being open is a choice you make. Holding back, on a conversation for example, is also a choice you make. Partial openness is akin to partial attention and partial involvement, and it is a choice. Consider your level of openness in all your relationships.

- **Appreciation:** Appreciation shows gratitude and recognises the significance or value you have taken from something another person has done for you. When you say 'please' and 'thank you' at home or at work, you automatically raise the other person's self-esteem. More formally, a written appreciation has more power than the spoken word. In business, relationships largely determine commercial success. Developing lifetime customers and shareholder loyalty is built on a foundation of trust, respect and good solid relationships. Again it is a learnable competency. How appreciative are you in your relationship?

iv. To Be Engaged In Purposeful Work

Making a significant contribution – a difference – in your chosen profession or career is what defines purposeful work. How worthwhile do you feel your work is? Has it a purpose that fits your talents? You are unlikely to reach your full potential unless you can name and appreciate your natural talents. When you work in harmony with your talents it's not work anymore, it's a mission or a cause with purpose. Ironically, your talents are often hiding in plain sight. You may bump into them regularly and still not appreciate them. To enjoy your work and do your best work, tap into your natural talents and turn them into superior competencies.

Many of the old definitions of success at work have changed over the last few decades. In the old days, companies offered the appealing prospect of a job-for-life. Loyalty and hard work were rewarded with job security and the prospects of climbing the corporate ladder. Today, quality of life issues and personal/professional growth opportunities are more powerful motivators among more highly educated employees. Furthermore, the knowledge worker must take greater personal responsibility for 'delivering' purposeful work and align this with the goals of the company.

The 'magnificent obsession' that drives the work pattern of many executives and business owners is the key to their success and, ironically, their failure. Business owners and managers often find themselves devoting the bulk of their time and energy to their business and much less quality time to family or personal life. Sadly, few seem to know how to regain the balance.

These managers work late evenings, travel frequently, entertain customers over dinner and take home full briefcases for the weekend. Even when they are 'not working', work often occupies their mind. They may be physically present at the family dinner table, for example, but their minds are miles away.

This becomes a vicious circle. All the motivation in terms of achievement, power, esteem and money comes from the work domain while the 'I'm doing it for the family' explanation seems a contradiction. The shock of a personal crisis – marriage break-up, early heart attack, child delinquency problems – often causes them to realise the consequences of their overwhelming focus on work.

The drive for mastery at work – this addiction type focus – and having a high quality personal and family life *is* achievable. But you must learn how to engage with this delicate imbalance. The things that made you successful up to now may not serve to keep you successful in the future. In fact, your strengths may become your weakness. Work life balance remains a challenge to be continuously considered. How do you manage this challenge?

There are two aspects to achieving balance between your personal and professional life. The balance between *who you are* and *what you do* is a mirror image of the home/work balance. To move from being a manager to being a leader requires an appreciation and an understanding of this transition.

First, you must be determined to learn the functional and technical competencies – *what you do* – which are 'learned' best practices to help you excel in your job. This is about your performance contribution and economic wellbeing. Professional competencies are often threshold, entry level, standards into a job or career and the more you climb the management ladder the less significant – probably 20 percent – your functionality matters. Technical, CV type accomplishments may help get you the job but they do not guarantee success.

Second, you must tap into your inborn leadership 'being' competencies to complete the picture at work. And, ironically, these are the 'secrets' to home success as well. Those are the character factors that differentiate your uniqueness and special personality traits from all others. These are about personal leadership and quality of life. Personal leadership competencies ensure your success at home, and at work. Self-actualisation requires you to balance both dimensions.

v. To Have Financial Freedom

Your ability to create personal and financial advantage is central to your success. Money has a bad reputation because most people don't have enough of it. To justify their lack, you will hear them say 'Money is the root of all evil' or 'Money can't buy happiness'. These ideas are often used to rationalise the failure to have money. Money is not the root of all evil, disastrous money management could be! In fact, money makes sense in a language all nations understand.

Do you want to be rich or wealthy? There's a big difference. There are a lot of pseudo symbols of richness, like the school or college you attended or the prestige attached to your occupation or the neighbourhood you live in. Rich can often be about level of income and be status oriented.

Being financially independent or wealthy, on the other hand, is building a lifetime asset. The best measure is your net worth. Net worth is the current value of your assets less your liabilities. Wealth generation requires an attitude of mind and is the result of a lifestyle of hard work, perseverance, planning and, most of all, self-discipline. The one-sentence key to financial success is 'Spend less than you make.' Wealth is not income. High income people make big money but also have big mortgages, heavy taxes and penal repayments.

Here is the harsh truth about wealth and financial freedom. Take any 100 men and women starting out in their career at 20 years of age. By 60, after 40 years of work, only one will be wealthy, four will be financially independent, five will continue to work out of necessity, 36 will have died, 54 will be dependent on social services and government support. To have financial freedom in your own lifetime is a very worthy goal which automatically allows you other freedoms such as the freedom to engage with the other ingredients of success as outlined. How much attention are you giving to your financial affairs?

vi. Self Actualisation: To Be Living A Full Life

The sixth ingredient of success is to embrace the idea that life is for living. Success is a journey, not a destination. Today, to be living on the outer edges of your potential means you must be a constant learner – always changing and growing. Always seeking out. Always listening. Always reading. Readers are learners. Readers are leaders. The natural tendency to get into a comfort zone paralyses this opportunity. So be aware of its danger. Self-actualisation or self-fulfilment is regarded as the highest motivator of mankind but it's always a precarious balancing act.

Could you be selling yourself short? How are your levels of self-confidence? Are you in control of your life? How good are you at your chosen work? Do you accept yourself, unconditionally, as a valuable and worthwhile human being? What is life all about for you? These are root cause questions that test your levels of self-actualisation.

If you are living the full life, it will be self-evident. Living life to the full and taking control of your own destiny can best be seen when you:

- Fully accept yourself, warts and all, as a valuable and worthwhile person

- Demonstrate the fullness of your personality without fear or inhibition

- Experiment with new things and boldly go where you would have shown reluctance previously

- Love your family and have quality relationships with people in general

- Perform well in your chosen career or business.

By practicing these recommendations, you put yourself on the road to self-actualisation where you can confidently 'ready yourself' to cross the rubicon.

Here are two considerations for you to reflect upon as you contemplate these success factors for yourself.

First, put as much effort into *who you are* as *what you do* in your journey of life before you decide *where you are going*. Take 100 percent responsibility for developing your own levels of self-esteem and self-confidence. Develop your inner potential. You are unique. Identifying and working with your natural and acquired talents in the direction of a worthwhile goal is as near to fulfilment as you are likely to get.

Second, learn how to be even more successful than you already are by following a proven success system. Any system is better than no system. Systems thinking can give you the success edge. Tens of thousands of men and women from all walks of life have transformed their lives by redefining their views of success and using a success system.

The mind-frames and activities that got you to where you are now may have served you well. How will these attitudes serve you in the future? No amount of success at work will compensate for distress at home. Don't become a prisoner of your commercial success at the expense of your peace of mind, health and close personal relationships. Spend some time reframing or reconsidering your concept of success as you prepare to cross your own rubicon.

Success is the most talked and written about subject in the world today. The bookshops are packed with 'how-to' success methodologies. Yet, it seems to still be quite an elusive subject in terms of how people understand it and, even more mysteriously, it apparently bypasses the majority of men and women by their own summation of it.

Defining success – or the concept of success – is the first step to mastering it. A thousand definitions are available in literature and presented by the success experts. But it's always personal to you and the six outlined in this success index are just a template to give you a benchmark.

'Success is a journey, not a destination' is a favourite definition for many people. You never quite get there because it's always an evolving process of change and becoming different and better.

'Success is setting and achieving your definite objectives' is another solid interpretation of the success concept. However, it's not just achieving things or reaching milestones but having the courage to set goals towards their achievement that is the key. Achieving things is automatic if you just live life. Achieving things that you purposefully set down in writing is the success code that most people miss out on.

Abraham Maslow, the psychologist, wrote "The ultimate aim of human life is to become everything you are capable of becoming". To reach your potential as a person can be dramatically improved by 'thinking strategy'.

Developing character may be the great aim of success if we follow what Goethe wrote in 1790 "Talent develops in quiet places, character in the full current of human life". Character is made up of the distinctive mental and moral qualities that you alone possess.

Shakespeare was surely referring to character when he wrote "To thine own self be true, and it must follow, as night the day, thou canst not be false to any man". Are integrity and a good reputation the ultimate measures of success? Shakespeare also wrote "Who steals my purse steals trash ... but he that filches from me my good name ... makes me poor indeed".

According to Sidney Jourard, the psychologist, 85 percent of your success in life will come from the quality of your relationships. The other 15 percent of your success will come from your achievements.

Phil Knight of Nike, creator of the 'Just Do It' slogan says "You only have to succeed the last time" to be successful. Failure and success go hand in hand.

Thomas Edison, inventor of the electric light bulb, failed over 10,000 times before finding the correct solution that lights the world. He regarded each failed experiment as just another step towards an inevitable successful outcome. He assumed that success was inevitable and just a matter of time.

Ralph Waldo Emerson sums up success in the epic words "A man becomes what he thinks about most of the time".

Get to grips with your own definition of success. Clarity and focus is essential for success. The fact of the matter is that you *deserve* to be successful. Often, you do not get what you want but what you *deserve*. The word *deserve* is derived from two Latin words *De* and *Servus* which mean 'from service'. So maybe success is about serving other people.

1.2 SCRIPTING THE CURRENT STATUS …WHAT IS YOUR OWN STORY?

The process of writing about the people and circumstances that you live and work with on a day to day basis can be very therapeutic. When you write free-hand in chunks of about 90 minutes you will tend to delve into areas that you only give scant time and mental attention to in normal circumstances.

Writing in an essay type format allows you empty your mind onto the page. It's been said that 'the faintest ink is better than the strongest memory'. In this exercise, you get to write your own story. Inhibition stops 95 percent of the population from embarking on this exercise. Or maybe it's their lack of awareness with regard to the power of free-writing. The forced response aspect of this puts enough pressure on you to get it going. Forced response means you respond because you 'force' yourself to risk your thoughts to paper. The tendency to do it when you have it all thought out is the rock you perish on in this kind of exercise. The rest is relatively easy, as you will find.

As you write, your explanatory style will emerge. You get to meet yourself on the page. Write with abandon. Write as you think and talk. The act of writing down your thoughts captures, in a concrete form, the very essence of *who you are* and *what you do*.

The two words no one else can say in the world about you are the words, 'I am'. So in this current situation review, use these two words or similar as much as you like. 'I am a father/mother of …, I live in …, I am 31 years old …, I earn …, I love …, I am stuck …, I am happy about …' An alternative or parallel consideration is to pick themes or topics in your life right now. There is no one-way or best way of doing this, just your way. This is *your* book, written *your* way. Consider what emerges, later. Many people are astonished at the emphasis or emotion given to one topic over another. Did you write positively or negatively about your current reality? Were you suggesting solutions to difficulties or just wallowing in the problem? Were you writing like a journalist giving commentary or were you giving recommendations to yourself?

If you were to go to a legal advisor with a complicated case the first thing he would advise you to do after your first briefing would be to write it all down. There is a power of legitimacy about words on a page that you cannot get by mere thought. A counsellor often encourages a client to write in a diary over an extended period of time to help bring clarity to the 'chatter-box' between their ears. Writing has power. The pen is mightier than the sword. So get scripting, or typing.

Reading, thinking, and writing go hand in hand in terms of scripting your current status. As far back as 1764, William Shenstone wrote that "The world is divided into people that read, people that write, people that think and foxhunters". A bit 'tongue in cheek' but true nevertheless. Reading, thinking and writing are the big three personal strategy concepts that you need to grasp at this stage of strategy formulation.

Reading about any aspect of strategy is like nourishment for your thinking. Readers are leaders. Readers are learners. Readers feed the mind with a multitude of ideas and creative inputs. The person who can read, and does not read, has no advantage over the person who cannot read. The statistics are frightening – the average manager reads less than one non-fiction book per year on their subject which is management, leadership, personal or professional development. Think of a book as the condensed wisdom of what someone else has learned. So, read extensively to more readily learn what may have taken the author a lifetime to learn. You can learn by your own mistakes and experience as you strategise or you can learn from the lessons of other people. Strategy intelligence is often the application of commonsense – "the one percent inspiration and 99 percent perspiration" – as Thomas Edison put it.

Thinking about thinking is a neglected process. Thinking on paper is a learned practice that improves the more reading and writing you do. "There is nothing either good or bad, but thinking makes it so" is the great line from Hamlet, one of Shakespeare's plays. Thinking on paper is writing. Systems thinking is better. System thinking is like having a platform or framework in place to 'grasp' your thoughts. Capturing your multitudinous thoughts is the challenge – otherwise you lose them into oblivion.

Writing improves with practice. Write as you think. Write as you talk. Write in free-flow. You can edit, design and beautify the script later. Writer's block happens to even the most experienced wordsmith. Imagine you are a dramatist or playwright rather than an informal scribbler as you pen your assessment of your current situation right now. John Keats wrote that "Fine writing is next to fine doing the top thing in the world". The process of starting your own fine writing process moves you from being operational to being strategic.

1.3 WHAT 'BUSINESS' ARE YOU IN? ... WHAT BUSINESS SHOULD YOU BE IN?

You are self-employed by virtue of the fact that you sell your services to your employer. In that sense, you run your own personal and professional services business. This state of mind is very powerful when you ask yourself the following questions: 'What business *am* I in? What business *should* I be in? What business *could* I be in?' The need to ask the question is even more important if you are currently a shareholder and business owner. Be careful you understand the context and power of the question to fully appreciate its value.

The question 'What business am I in?' seems at first sight to have answers that are simple and obvious. I am in the retail or banking or education or transport business. But the term 'business' has wider connotations in personal strategy. As a noun, the word *'business'* is defined in the dictionary as 'a person's regular occupation or trade' or 'work to be done or matters to be attended to'. So, in this latter context, consider what *'business'* you are about. If someone said to you "Okay, it's a go, we are in business" what would it mean? In the Bible Jesus said "I am about my Father's business". What does it mean to 'mind your own business'?

With regard to your life and work, you can now ask yourself some questions such as: 'What business am I in and how do I excel? Who is my customer? What are my critical success factors? What are my core competencies? What is my calling? What competencies will I need in three years time?' Use basic business parameters as if you were self-employed to answer these questions. If you are already self-employed or an investor push out the possibilities inherent in the question from a personal and professional perspective.

As you can see, asking and answering this question tends to provide many different perspectives and valuable personal insights. Remember, in personal strategy, one moment of insight can be worth a lifetime of experience. Just asking the question can 'force' you to re-think or reconsider your positioning.

Failure to clarify 'What business am I in?' applies in the classic example of the owners of the American railways at the start of the 20th century. They considered themselves to be in the railroad business rather than the transportation industry. They therefore failed to capture new customers as railroad usage decreased and road/air transport became more popular. IBM nearly went bankrupt because it missed the computer software business revolution. Ray Kroc of McDonalds said he was "not in the hamburger business", he was in the real estate business. Microsoft adjusted itself just in time to become the force they are today. Coca Cola have redefined the business they are in from the soft drinks industry which they have dominated to the wider drinks market where they see all drinks – water, tea, coffee – as their potential market.

When Century Management was set up in 1989, it was in the management training business and our customers were small and medium business owners. Now, however, the answers to 'What business are we in?' and 'Who are our customers?' have changed considerably. We are now in the cultural transformation, performance improvement, strategy consulting and organisation development business. We provide strategic change management solutions. We provide systems, techniques and know-how to solve business problems. Our corporate slogan is *Creating Business Advantage*.

Interviewed in Fortune magazine, April 2006, Rob Carter of Federal Express, when asked 'what business are FedEx in?' said "I believe we engineer time … as the world shrinks and changes". Remember, clarity and focus are huge concepts in strategy. FedEx are always clear and very focused.

What business *should* you be in? Think laterally, think strategically about this question for yourself. Are you in the business of making ends meet or putting bread on the table? Are you in the business of the product your company sells or the profession you qualified in? Or are you in the business of adding-value, solving problems, getting results, making money, growing teams, growing assets, master-minding projects and growing revenues?

Individuals are like companies, in that they become so busy coping with today's operational demands and meeting staff and customer needs that they fail to invest thinking time and other resources into exploring possibilities in other areas. As the CEO of your own private professional services company consider these points:

- What are you really good at and how are you aligning those talents to the needs of your business?

- Where do you see yourself and your business in three years time? In five years time?

- What are the trends in your professional marketplace?

- How are your competitors (colleagues) doing? How easy is it to enter a new market (change profession, move company, move industry)?

- How are you positioned within your market (company/industry) and with your professional competitors?

- When is a new idea the latest fad or the start of a new trend? Are you keeping up-to-date? Ahead? Behind?

- Why do some people (your competitors), who are apparently in your business, get rewarded better than you do? And much greater rewards? Are they in the same business as you?

One manager explained he was in the business of 'getting the job done'. Another said he was in the business of 'developing managers into leaders to achieve extraordinary levels of accomplishment'. Another said she was in the business of 'adding-value and consistently getting the results required'. Another clearly positioned himself as 'a profit improvement specialist' and focused all his efforts on demonstrating how to improve the bottom line. A life insurance salesman told me he was in the 'peace of mind' business.

What business could you be in? What jobs or career are you preparing for? Remember, the job for life is over. You may have to think about 'attend to' a whole new career by the time you are 30 or start a new career at 58 in today's ever changing world.

Could you be self-employed for example? Could you be an investor in other people's ideas? Could you be a turnaround manager in struggling companies? Could you be a social worker in Africa? Could you be a politician? Could you establish yourself as an expert or an authority on your preferred area of excellence? Could you be a portfolio worker or investor earning your livelihood from several sources?

What is your positioning? What is your 30-second differentiation statement? What business are you really in? Should you be in? Could you be in? What's your real job? Think strategically.

1.4 SIX RESOURCES ANALYSIS ... HOW RESOURCEFUL ARE YOU?

You have six critical resources – just like a business – that overlap and interlink and that you juggle with daily. Your ability to deploy these resources for your maximum advantage will be a critical factor in your personal and professional strategy. If you view these six resources as a 'chain-of-resources', then the concept of *'a chain is as strong as its weakest link'* comes into play.

Many people find it difficult to identify the weakest link in their chain-of-resources and, indeed, frequently fix the wrong problem. Most people, ironically, have the solutions to their own problems within their own capability and, unfortunately, they don't appreciate the impact of their weakest link on their overall performance or potential. Your weak link is never isolated. It has an impact on the whole system. A chain **is** as strong as the weakest link. The six links in your chain of resources are: Money, Product, Physical, Intangible, Time and People. Assume that everyone who is not reaching their full potential has a weak link in one or more of these resources.

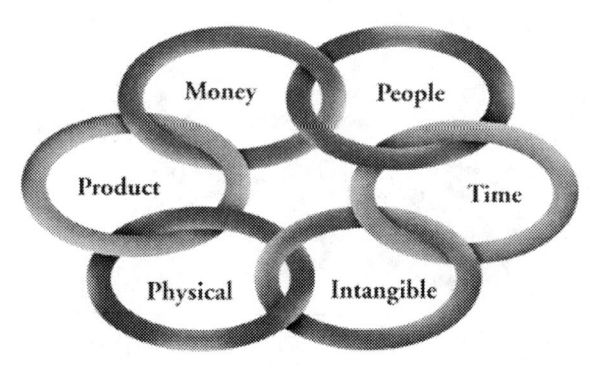

Figure 1.4a Six Resources Analysis: Which Is Your Weakest Link?

Imagine you had an annoying health problem and felt unwell for several months. You had pains in your back, shoulder, neck and legs. You put these problems down to influenza, long hours at work and being physically run down. You visited several doctors who could not diagnose exactly the source of your ailment. Some even gave you treatment. Eventually one doctor diagnosed the source of your sickness and immediately sent you to hospital for the removal of gallstones. Within two weeks you were feeling better. Within two months your whole system — physiological and mental — was operating at 100 percent. Your weak link or choke point or limiting factor (gallstones, in this case) had been removed.

A choke point – weak link – is a constraint or an obstacle that limits best performance or the easy movement from one point to another along the least line of resistance. It has the effect, eventually, of slowing down best performance within your system.

Your ability to identify, strengthen or remove the weakness link in your chain-of-resources will probably be your most important task of the year in terms of creating a personal strategy. By eliminating one choke point, you may free up all other parts of your processes and systems.

One weak link in your chain of resources can weaken, render ineffective or destroy your best laid plans. Most people are unsure where to look for their weakest link, just as most businesses have developed a 'functional blindness' to their own defects. They're just too near the problem. The simplicity of this concept may account for the fact that it is so often overlooked as a personal or business improvement solution.

Figure 1.4b A chain is as strong as its weakest link

In terms of business results, what determines superior performance in your workplace? Why are there profitable companies in unprofitable industries? Apply the same kind of questioning to your personal and professional strategy. Why do some people earn far more than their colleagues, all things being equal? Why do some people under-perform and others consistently perform 'out of their skin'. What separates the best from the rest? Why are some people more successful than others?

What are your talents? What are your drivers? What is your potential? What are your limitations? What's stopping you? Answers to these questions may be found in a resource-based view of your current situation analysis. Let's review each of the resources to help you identify your choke points in the following sections.

i. THE MONEY RESOURCE

'Money makes the world go round' and 'money is the source of all evil' are the two divergent perspectives on this first resource. Money is the most obvious and misunderstood of all the resources. Of course, our ability to work towards creating higher and higher levels of financial independence is central to personal strategy.

Why is it that only one percent of the population are truly wealthy, only four percent are financially independent which means they could live without ever having to work again, 15 percent have some savings at retirement, and 80 percent of the population are dependent on pensions, still working or broke at retirement? How could this be in one of the richest countries in the world? Why does every first world country have the same dreadful statistics?

"Early to bed and early to rise helps make a person healthy, wealthy and wise" is a time-honoured proverb that seems to have run into some difficulty in the modern world. Health, wealth and wisdom are elusive ideals for the majority of people, especially wealth creation. The World Health Organisation informs us that anxiety and depression will be the number one disease in the world by 2010.

Despite the fact that Ireland is one of the wealthiest countries in the world, about 23 percent of the Irish population are living 'at risk' of poverty and as high as 72 percent of workers are unhappy going to work every day. Figures are similar in America and Europe. So, while health, wealth and happiness are still the big three aspirations that most people seek in their lives all three seem to be falling well short of expectations.

We will explore aspects of money management in other places in this book because it is central to your strategic success. The money resource has very little to do with luck and everything to do with other basics as we shall see.

ii. THE PRODUCT RESOURCE

The second major resource to consider is the product resource. In the business world 'a product' may be a single article or substance manufactured or refined for sale. A product may also be the actual product with packaging and design. A further dimension may be the augmented product with delivery, guarantees and service. A product, in other words, is a major resource of any commercial business or non-business organisation.

Have you ever considered yourself as 'a product'? Do you feel your character has been formed by a particular period of time or situation? In the sense that 'everyone serves someone' and 'everyone sells something' you are a product. You could be a product of your time or circumstance like the 'baby boomers' of the 1960s. You could be a product of professional parents who live in a cash-rich, time-poor economy. In his book, *The Pope's Children: Ireland's New Elite*, author David McWilliams asks us "To meet the new Irish generation, born either side of the Pope's visit (1979) who have been squeezed into the middle and lifted up by the Celtic Tiger". With regard to how you see yourself as a product resource, consider these questions:

- How well do you position yourself?
- What is your unique selling proposition?
- Why are you on the payroll?
- How valuable is the contribution you make?
- Who are your customers?
- How well branded are you?
- What is your 'sell by date'?
- What stage of the product lifecycle are you at right now?

In classic marketing strategy 'product' takes pride of place. In personal strategy 'you' are the product. Consider yourself as a resource with talents and capabilities that can be deployed to add-value and benefit to some enterprise.

Marketing professionals rarely talk about what a product *is*, but rather what it *does*. Consider then, the benefits and the added-value *you* deliver to whomever you serve. Consider the problems *your* product solves! Consider the added-value *you* deliver!

In that real sense you are like a business product. Your uniqueness and potential has to be realised and packaged. Every product on earth is only as good as the perceived need it fulfils. You must, however, position yourself not as a raw commodity-like product, but as a portfolio solution provider who brings benefits, value and results. Products do things for people and they have shape and size. A solutions provider takes a consultant or doctor approach to what they deliver. Different terminology is used to position you as a solutions provider. It's more conceptual and expertise based.

Your reputation with yourself is as important as your reputation with other people in terms of personal strategic positioning. How do you 'stand' in the eyes of your colleagues, partners or customers? How would they 'sum you up' as a professional? Are you a manager who gets things done or a leader who gets exceptional performance from other ordinary people? If you are a sales professional, do you position yourself as a mere seller of products or as a 'doctor' with solutions to solve customer problems? The former just sells products. The latter consults, listens, matches needs and wants, offers solutions and befriends their customer. Do you position yourself as an obvious expert in your field who adds-value and expertise at every opportunity or are you just the same as everyone else? By the way, everyone sells and everyone has customers. Positioning is 'everything' with strategy.

iii. THE PHYSICAL RESOURCE

The third resource is the physical resource. Resources were traditionally seen by economists as land, labour and capital. Land was the primary physical resource and as you know more wars have been fought over territorial rights than for any other reason. Timber, coal, iron and, more recently, oil and gas are the by-products of the land resource. These resources stimulated the growth of the manufacturing industry, transport, trade and agriculture. Today, the physical resource is more broadly defined. In business and as a personal strategist it is made up of three primary elements, the place or location you live, the equipment you use and technology. Let's look at each in turn.

First, your home and office – where you conduct your daily activities – are an important resource in your personal strategy. Any good estate agent will name three primary considerations when buying property – location, location, location. Yet it's not just location. It's how you present your location.

Never present your office in a bad light. Good marketing and good communications are best measured by the response they get. Your job as a personal strategist is to create perceptions of unique added-value in the minds of your customers, and one of your most important customers is your boss. Other customers are your colleagues or support teams. Suppliers and professional service providers are other customers.

If you are a business owner, for example, you set the standard in terms of how you manage your premises in terms of occupancy, maintenance cost, rental income and geographical suitability. Your best competitor sets the benchmark for quality, prices and service standards.

Your office, however, presents unique opportunities to differentiate yourself. If my first impression, largely determined by my visual inspection, is that your office is shabby or disorganised, then I would tend to conclude, from even small observations, that your service will be shabby and disorganised too.

That's how perception works, fairly or unfairly. Perception is the reality. Beware. Customers easily jump to conclusions. Take personal control of this resource.

Successful businesses with excellent products, excellent people and excellent financial management systems sabotage themselves by poor presentation of their businesses. For example, by painting the exterior of the office, updating the external signage, cleaning up the car park, redesigning the reception area you may totally change customer perceptions. Quality and speed may have been key variables in competitive advantage in the 1980s and 1990s. Presentation and design are the 21st century winning-edge variables.

So, take control of your desk at the minimum. Take control of your dress, grooming and personal image. Your car can be a 'place' for many executives today. How is it presented on both the inside and outside?

Second, today's tools and equipment are designed to do everything better, faster, cheaper, easier, newer and different. Wireless technology and electronic commerce mean instant access and immediate connection. But, do you have the equipment and technological resources to deliver *what you do* in a faster, better or easier way? Could the use of obsolete equipment be your choke point? If so, what can you do about it?

Equipment today is definitely more efficient, speedier and robust. But how does it serve you to get that strategic edge? Managers everywhere are overwhelmed, working longer hours and more disorganised. Most don't use even basic technologies to overcome their day to day problems.

Third, technology is a key physical resource. The massive computer capability in most organisations lies dormant. Lack of investment in training and time to explore the current capabilities of your technology may mean that your computers are an under-utilised asset.

In most cases, it simply means reading the manuals and maximising the capability of the software. Invest time and explain your specific needs to a software specialist. In today's better, faster, cheaper, easier world, obsolete computer equipment and out-of-date computer software should not be your choke points.

In earlier times, land was the key physical resource and became the power symbol for individuals and nations. Labour, ironically, was also seen as a physical resource in that a person was seen as a 'lifter and shifter' – a bit like a machine is seen today. Natural physical resources like coal, timber and steel also dominated economic life ... but not anymore. The dominance of the physical resource may be over – except for oil and gas – but it still plays an important part in the balance of all the resources.

iv. THE INTANGIBLE RESOURCE

The intangible resource – the fourth resource – can be the most valuable resource in today's economy. It can produce long term results far greater than your original investment in it. Whether as a business or a personal concept, the intangible resource is better understood as an abstract construct. You can't feel it. You can't taste it. You can only measure its effects. High morale, esprit de corps, motivation, respect, brand, recognition, knowledge and intellectual capability, character, philosophy and ethos, image and goodwill may be regarded as intangibles in the business world, but they can also apply perfectly to your personal strategy analysis. Consider three aspects of the intangible resource – knowledge, talent and image – as follows:

You can't physically see knowledge but you can measure its effectiveness. It does or doesn't result in increased productivity and results. How does your own knowledge-barometer work? Are you well-read and current? Do you have experience or expertise? Are you a knowledge expert? Could you be an authority in your field?

You can't touch talent in the physical sense but you can measure its effects by the reputation you hold and the superior results you generate. How much investment have you put into fine-tuning your natural behaviours, skills and attributes into 'talents' that produce consistently excellent performance?

Likewise, you cannot readily see image or goodwill but you can measure its effects by the trust others place on you. How trustworthy are you? How does 'brand you' score? Have you invested in a personal brand building exercise? Get a reputation as a trustworthy person and everything is possible. Doors will be opened for you. Lenders will give you money. And customers will gratefully pay you higher fees for your service rendered.

Knowledge and talent have become the most important factors in personal economic life and foremost of all the intangibles. Talent may well be the key wealth creator of the 21st century. Effective knowledge and talent management need to be turned into core competencies. You must invest time and money to develop those competencies necessary for you to deliver superior results. Learn the new thinking, techniques, skills, framework and expertise to make this happen. Transform your capacity to create, classify, apply, exploit and value your talent and knowledge to improve performance.

Intellectual capital is defined by Thomas A. Stewart in his book *Intellectual Capital* as 'intellectual material – knowledge, information, intellectual property, experience, expertise – that can be put to use to create wealth'. It is your brainpower. It is an intangible resource like no other.

Knowledge management is about fuelling this capital so that it becomes a catalyst for change, innovation, motivation and personal/business advantage. In the industrial age, land, natural resources (coal, timber, etc.), human and machine labour were the ingredients from which wealth was created. In this new age of information and communication, wealth is the product of knowledge. Therefore you must become a knowledge manager and an obvious expert in your field to gain the advantage. Becoming an expert who delivers a value-added service is a difficult to imitate strategy for your competitors.

Everybody has talents, but most people do not know what their talents are. When you ask them, they respond in terms of subject knowledge. In other words, most people focus on *what they do*, instead of identifying their talents and developing the skills that go with talent to achieve positive and sustainable results.

For most people their talents are hiding in plain sight, but so interwoven into the fabric of their personality they can be hard to detect. However, talents do leave tracks and can be identified and developed. There are definite methods of turning talent into consistently excellent performance. This can be done by benchmarking, measuring and developing the critical competencies necessary for superior performance and results in the position you hold in your company. This holds true even if you are a business owner.

Your personal brand is one of your most powerful intangible resources. It can be one of the most visible and powerful statements and actions you can make about your present set-up and the future direction of your career. It was a branding consultant, Walter Landor, who said that "Products are made in the factory, brands are made in the mind".

Investment in your identity that, in turn, enhances your professional reputation yields one of your greatest returns on all personal investments. Everyone has an identity. It's what you present to the world. Image, on the other hand, is the perception your 'public' — customers, suppliers, the community, shareholders, bankers — receive from your identity. Identity is made up of brand, colour, reputation, behaviours, culture, history, style, standards, values, quality and character.

Identity management is the way you manage the interactions and transactions between you and your various stakeholders. You manage them rather than let them unfold in an unsystematic way. How you want the world to perceive you and how you present yourself is your identity. Identity communicates four things about you: *who you are, what you do, how you do it, what you represent.*

With regard to the intangible resource, your foremost questions are: 'How do you continually create personal strategic advantage and are you harnessing knowledge, talent and brand as drivers of advantage for you?' Intangible assets are as valuable as tangible assets because you cannot produce results without them. You will find that the reason you are not realising your potential has quite a lot to do with how you utilise your intangible resources.

v. THE TIME RESOURCE

The time resource is the fifth resource. Henry Austin Dobson wrote in *The Paradox of Time* in 1877 that "Time goes, you say? Ah no! Alas, Time stays, we go." There are 168 hours in every week. Everyone gets exactly the same number of hours. There are, on average, 2,000 work hours per year. How do you utilise them? Now complete this exercise: Write down your age on a page. Multiply by 365 for the number of days in the year. Then multiply again by 24 for the number of hours in a day. The figure is the number of hours you have lived to date.

Now, subtract that figure from 703,428 if you are a woman and 657,876 if you are a man. These are the life expectancy figures in Ireland. To be precise, the figures are 80.3 years for a woman and 75.1 years for a man. Now consider the merits of investing about 100 hours on this rubicon exercise. In the overall context of life, it's not a lot of time is it? Time is precious. The famous last words of Elizabeth I in 1603 were reputed to have been "All my possessions for a moment of time".

One of your biggest challenges in this cash-rich time-poor age is your ability to embrace and control time by appreciating just how vital the time resource is in maximising your potential. Could the management of time be your own personal weak link? Could it be an organisational problem where you work?

More than 80 percent of managers and business owners regard the management of time as their biggest single challenge. Because there is a constant supply of this resource, it is probably one of the most abused resources in the six link chain of business resources.

Is time your choke point? Is it the reason that you fail to rectify other choke points in building your personal wealth, getting a balance in your home-work life or building the competencies to leverage you forward? Consider time.

Appreciate time. Back in the 19th century, Dion Boucicault wrote "Men talk of killing time, while time is quietly killing them".

Is it the reason that your communication is not so good and is it a contributing factor to your low morale, low trust or high stress levels? Is there a connection between low levels of creativity, innovation, common sense and initiatives being taken? How much time do you give to personal planning per month or per year? Are you now prepared to invest 100 hours on this Rubicon exercise? At work, is there a connection between excessive wastage, high staff turnover, low sales and poor profits?

Many managers constantly moan that they haven't got enough time or there are never enough hours in the day. Time, of course, is not the problem – it's how you use it that's the problem. Time is the most predictable resource for you as a manager. It has a fixed amount and a fixed rate of expenditure. However, once used, it is irretrievable. Remember, everyone is a manager of their own affairs.

Decide to become a time management expert after your current situation analysis by listening to CDs, tapes, reading books and attending courses on the better use of time. Go beyond the diary organisers to a total, integrated implementation system. Remember always, the words of C. Northcote Parkinson who coined the famous words in 1958 and which became known as 'Parkinson's Law': "Work expands so as to fill the time available".

In your time assessment, keep in mind it's your responsibility to use your time better. If you find yourself making excuses for yourself or blaming other people or circumstances, then you have not grasped the first essential of excellent time management which is to take 100 percent responsibility for making things happen.

In Macbeth, Shakespeare struggled with time like everyone else: "If you can look into the seeds of time, and say which grain will grow and which will not". Whether the objective is business process reengineering, professional development or to implement cultural change, you need to remind yourself of Key Result Areas (KRAs) all the time and book time with yourself to make your KRAs happen. The logic is blindingly obvious – the things you lose sight of are not remembered and therefore you do nothing about them. Distraction is everywhere. You major on minors and you lose focus. You need to 'visually' see, on an everyday basis, your KRAs.

vi. THE PEOPLE RESOURCE

The sixth link in the six-link chain of resources is the people resource. The other resources – money, product, physical, intangible and time – make things possible. People make things happen.

Ultimately, you are in the 'people business'. Yet here you are likely to find your biggest choke point in terms of self-limitations, interpersonal relationships and your ability to maximise the potential of your team. These choke points are usually psychological and cultural rather than technical and physical.

A physical choke point, such as on a production line, the design of a product, a building or a piece of equipment can be physically removed and re-engineered. Time and money are lost at an incredible rate in some organisations. Wastage can be as high as 30 percent of total sales revenues in the worst companies. There are people implications at all levels. It is often hard to measure – and difficult to prove – the cause of the bad effects that lead to poor resource management and it is therefore difficult to quantify its down-side.

Emotional, psychological and cultural choke points, however, which are embedded deep within a person's psyche are even more difficult to identify and eliminate. All too often, unfortunately, they are not dealt with in any meaningful way.

One of the major choke points for an individual is a lack of personal empowerment – a lack of self-confidence and self-belief. Most people in the workforce today believe that they are limited in some way and therefore probably only perform to about 50 percent of their capability. The cause of their own inadequate performance has more to do with their mental makeup than lack of opportunities, skills, knowledge or any external factors.

Most people have only a vague idea of how to unlock their own potential and be thoroughly fulfilled in their personal and career development. This is the root cause of low performance, frustration, absenteeism and dissatisfaction with work and career development. It leads to stress, mental illness and family problems.

The human being is a success being and is only really fully motivated when working towards personal, career or business goal attainment.

Unfortunately, most people have only a vague idea (or no idea) of how to unlock their success system. They don't know how to dismantle the block to progress along the road to their personal and professional development. This road-block or choke point impacts on all other developments.

FLYING IN FORMATION WITH THE SIX RESOURCES

Crossing the rubicon is emotional strategy in action. It challenges you to sort out your own thinking and purpose. Only then can you add real value to other people. The logic is very simple: The more you are 'fixed' and have clarity and focus the more you have to give to other people.

As part of your personal and professional strategic review, you learn to juggle the six resources of money, product, physical, intangible, time and people so that they 'fly in formation'. You learn to identify the choke points within the resources. You focus your attention, energies and other resources on eliminating the choke points. You realise that this may take three or four attempts on different resources and that you may need to get outside help. Your job is to maximise the output from these resources. The bottom-line today is always the outcome, the result.

The six resource model gives you a framework for prioritising and classifying your resources. Your intangibles are less likely to be copied than your more visible and accessible tangible resources. How can someone copy your personal brand? They may therefore be the key to sustainable talent management and building personal strategic advantage – to differentiating you. Keep thinking as a self-employed business owner, running your own professional services company.

Resources do not give you 'the winning edge' on their own. They are only good when strategically applied. You must act as the catalyst to convert them into something of value. You must first identify them. Then develop and protect them. Finally, you must effectively deploy them in your marketplace to create sustainable personal and professional advantage.

1.5 STRATEGIES FOR FINANCIAL INDEPENDENCE … HOW DO YOU BECOME WEALTHY?

"I've been rich and I've been poor" said the singer Pearl Bailey "and rich is better". Consider again the question: Do you want to be rich or wealthy?

'Rich' has overtones of status like the school or college you attended or the prestige attached to your occupation or the neighbourhood you live in or the Rolex you wear. High-income rich people may make above average money but also have big mortgages, heavy taxes and penal repayments. They are often prisoners of a high standard lifestyle. Rich can be more about lifestyle perceptions than economic reality.

'Wealth' is more about building a lifetime asset rather than current earned income. Building asset value and net worth are the best measures. Wealth is not just earned income. Wealth is more about generating passive cash flow from alternative sources to build parallel financial assets. Making money work for you rather than you working for money just about sums it up. Intelligently using other people's money – bankers – to build assets often defines good debt from bad debt. Good debt builds asset value wealth by gearing up assets over time.

i. FOUR CATEGORIES OF INCOME GENERATION

There are four categories of income generation that virtually everyone fits into: Full Time Employee, Self-Employed/Sole Trader, Company Owner/Director, Investor. You already fit into at least one of these categories. In Ireland, for example, business owners/proprietary directors can accumulate large profits in a company and pay corporation tax at 12.5 percent. Pension plans, tax shelters and property tax incentive schemes reduce the pain, for the rich and wealthy, of paying high taxes. The front page headline in *The Irish Times,* on 27th June 2006, sums it up nicely: "43 people earning over €1m paid under 5% tax".

Investors, of course, live off income from their assets (rental income, interest, share dividends) and don't need 'a job' in the normal way to live. This is true wealth in action. Creating wealth has been a prime motivator for mankind since time began. Anatole France wrote in 1908 that "In every well-governed state, wealth is a sacred thing; in democracies it is the only sacred thing." The mystery – or is it a mystery – is why so few men and women are truly wealthy.

The twin question for you to consider is 'Which category are you in now – Full Time Employee, Self-Employed/Sole Trader, Company Owner/Director, Investor – and which option will you be operating in, say, five years time?' What about 10 years time? You may, of course, have a preferred mix of all these options. Using all the figures here as a kind of benchmark, consider these questions:

- How much income – cashflow – do you need to pay your projected expenses when you choose to retire?
- What does your net worth (cash-concentrating) need to be to earn the passive income you need?
- When – what year – do you want to make the transition? Better still, pick one day – five, 10, 20 years out – and name it as your financial freedom day. Remember, strategy is about clarity and focus above all else.
- Financial freedom arrives when you reach the stage where your passive income – money earned without working – exceeds your expenses. Earned incomes become a bonus at this stage.

Albert Einstein once said "The hardest thing in the world to understand is income tax". The majority of taxpayers are confused by the tax system. Wealthy people, however, play the tax game superbly by building up enough assets to generate sufficient income to support themselves. The objective is to legitimately gain tax relief and benefit as an investor and therefore minimise the amount they pay to the Exchequer. The bottom line is that the pay as you earn employees and the self employed (to a lesser extent) are almost fully caught in the tax net and typically pay marginal tax at 42 percent and five percent PRSI in Ireland. Similar figures apply in most OECD economies.

ii. How to Get the Luck Factor with Money

People argue that wealthy people are 'lucky'. Luck, however, has been defined as '**L**abour **U**nder **C**orrect **K**nowledge'. It is when preparation meets opportunity. An English nobleman once said "A self-made man is one who believes in luck and sends his son to Oxford". In other words you make your own luck. When 'your luck is in' you are considered fortunate. When 'you try your luck' you attempt something risky. 'Worse luck' is a term of regret when you miss out on an opportunity. These terms can confuse the real essence of luck.

CROSSING THE RUBICON: Seven Steps To Writing Your Own Personal Strategy

"Being lucky is a matter of perception" according to a group of scientists lead by Dr. Matthew Smith at Liverpool Hope University. Their Luck Project team conducted experiments which lead to the conclusions that luck does not pick you. You choose to be lucky by your outlook and attitude to life. In other words, you are not born lucky or unlucky. Lucky men and women are skilled at noticing, creating and acting upon chance opportunities. They are better at networking and generally having a relaxed attitude to life. They expect good things to happen and turn 'bad luck into good' by, for example, considering how a bad incident could have been worse. According to Smith's research, lucky people tend to listen a lot more to their intuition and gut feeling, and act accordingly. Many people believe that luck is some kind of supernatural coincidence but Professor Simon Singh – a member of the Luck Project – points out that coincidences, from a mathematical perspective, are often predictable or even inevitable.

Luck is really a matter of probability. There is a probability that virtually anything can happen and you can personally increase or decrease the likelihood of something happening or not happening. For example, there is a probability that you could be killed in a car accident, but you can reduce this probability enormously by not driving after taking drink, driving within the speed limits and wearing a seatbelt.

There is a five percent probability that you will become a millionaire in the course of your lifetime. On the flip side, there is a 95 percent probability, according to all the current statistics, that you will not save one million euro in your lifetime. However, the law of averages dictates that luck is a function of the number of things you try. If you put yourself 'in harms way', and try more things more often, the luckier you get. Louis Pasteur once wrote that "Chance favours the prepared mind". Chance, risk and commitment seem to go hand in hand. Without commitment there is hesitation, the chance to draw back, always ineffectiveness.

Crossing the rubicon is about making financial decisions that change your modus operandi and attitude, forever. In terms of managing your resources, your goal is to become financially independent – even wealthy. Financial independence today probably means a net worth of several million euro and being wealthy means €3million plus. Remember, a millionaire today is not what it used to be!

Wealthy people have been interviewed, studied and observed exhaustively and one of the best books on the subject has sold more than three million copies. In the best selling book *The Millionaire Next Door* (1998), Thomas Stanley and William Danko point out that 'Those who look rich, and those who are rich' can be very different, and say that most people have it all wrong about how you become wealthy. They say that 80 percent of America's millionaires are first generation rich. After studying millionaires for more than 20 years, they discovered that millionaires have a lifestyle – the luck factor? – conducive to accumulating money under the following seven denominators:

- They Live Well Below Their Means: Many of them are in ordinary businesses such as welding contractors, auctioneers and dry cleaners. They drive ordinary cars. They are planners and meticulous budgeters. Their national anthem is frugal, frugal, frugal. Webster's Dictionary defines *frugal* as 'behaviour characterised by or reflecting economy in the use of resources'. A wasteful or lavish lifestyle is its opposite.

- They Allocate Their Time, Energy And Money Efficiently In Ways Conducive To Building Wealth: They invest wisely and employ professional money managers. Their goals are to educate their children, pay their taxes and retire comfortably. They spend nearly 20 times the number of hours planning their financial affairs than the average person spends, and they see a strong connection between investment planning and wealth accumulation.

- They Chose The Right Occupation: They know that the best paid people and the wealthiest in the world are the self-employed who love what they do. They believe money should never change your values. Making money is only a report card. It's a way to tell how you're doing.

- They Believe That Financial Independence Is More Important Than Displaying High Social Status: They live in middle-class neighbourhoods and wear ordinary clothes, watches and accessories and believe you aren't what you drive. Their motto is 'If your goal is to become financially secure, you're likely to attain it ... but if your motive is to make money, to spend money on a good life ... you're not going to make it'.

- **Their Parents Did Not Provide Economic Outpatient Care:** They teach their children to fish, rather than giving them fish. They realise that children who receive an easy handout from their well-off parents may well lose out in the long term. Rich children often feel their parent's capital is their income ... just waiting for them to spend it.

- **Their Adult Children Are Economically Self-Sufficient:** Most are surprised to realise that their parents are wealthy. They continually teach their children frugality and rarely talk about inheritance or the gifts their children will receive after they die. They stay out of their adult children's family matters. They tell their children that there are lots of things more valuable than money.

- **They Are Proficient In Targeting Market Opportunities:** Why is it that you're not wealthy? Perhaps it's because you are not following a niche in the market and specialising in delivering a service to that sector. The millionaire next door does!

iii. THREE LEVELS OF WEALTH

The answer to the question "Why do the rich get richer and the poor get poorer" has intrigued me for more than 20 years and having researched the subject exhaustively I have come up with some conclusions.

Let's consider who are the wealthy few in Ireland and, more importantly, how do they become wealthy? Wealth management bankers outline three divisions or levels of wealth.

First, are the **Mass Affluent**. There are probably between 100,000-200,000 'ordinary' millionaires in Ireland, when the asset values of private homes are considered. Many are accidental millionaires because of their property-based wealth. In America, according to their IRS, there are more than seven million millionaires, 300 billionaires and some 50 trillionaires. In fact, a millionaire is created every four minutes in America with more than 100,000 new millionaires being created every year. The 'Irish Dream' has only caught fire during the Celtic Tiger era from 1995 and proves that the American dream is possible anywhere. The Irish population now has 600,000 men and women in their late 50s and 60s who may well represent the first Irish leisured class, many of whom have down-traded their family homes at exorbitant gains. These are jokingly called the 'worried wealthy'. Germany had such a well off retired class 50 years ago.

Who wants to be a millionaire? Some might argue that they are two a penny these days – the Irish National Lottery alone has created almost 300. Many Dublin homeowners could also call themselves millionaires. Of course, they would have to sell their property to realise that value.

Second, are **High Net Worth Individuals**. There are 30,000 High Net Worth Individuals (HNWIs) in Ireland in the category of €2-25 million, and they constitute the real core of wealthy Ireland. Wealth managers estimate there are 300 individuals in Ireland who have an average net worth of €50 million each while another 3,000 have between €10-50 million each in assets. In Britain, more than 20,000 people are estimated to have assets in excess of €6 million. However, joining the rich club is a good deal harder than 25 years ago when you take inflation into account. Comparing the consumer price index for 1980 and today you could buy three times as much 25 years ago.

Traditionally, millionaires were seen as people who did not have to work and could live off their assets. Coutts bank in England estimates you could need an income of £355,000 with assets of £1,236,000 to live in such a lifestyle. In Ireland, the millionaire figure is about €3.2 million based on the Coutts estimates.

Contrary to popular perception, the beneficiaries of the Celtic Tiger boom have not just been the self-employed, business owners and investors. Salaried employees have dramatically improved their income potential. In 2001, for example, 6,500 self-employed earned between €100,000 – 200,000. In 2005 the figure was 12,500. However, the figures for salaried employees earning between €100,000-200,000 dramatically increased from 11,300 in 2001 to 44,500 in 2005. The Celtic Tiger gone wildly mad!

Let's take a few live examples from a survey in April 2006. Managing Directors averaged out at €167,000 with the highest being €468,000 and the lowest €50,000. According to a survey in the *Sunday Independent* (April 30th 2006), the average pay and perks of an Irish CEO running a public company topped €1.2 million in 2005. An executive director of an Irish plc averaged out at €815,000. The average management accountant in Dublin earns €81,000 per annum according to Dr. Tony White, Director of the Chartered Institute of Management Accountants in Ireland. Keep in mind that the average industrial wage is €29,300 and one of the highest in the world. All these figures should help benchmark where you stand in the money stakes.

Over 600 people (300 employed and 300 self-employed) earned over €1 million in 2005. The diagram below, from the Central Statistics Office, explains the Irish salary surge in graphic detail over a five year period.

Gross Income	2001	2002	2003	2004	2005
€1-10,000	489,700	397,200	385,800	375,000	363,200
€10,000 - 20,000	493,700	394,400	385,000	372,300	357,700
€20,000 - 30,000	280,900	332,800	343,700	351,300	352,200
€30,000 - 40,000	147,700	206,500	222,200	241,500	253,100
€40,000 - 50,000	73,900	128,200	138,600	153,600	165,300
€50,000 - 70,000	59,400	125,600	138,300	158,500	177,800
€70,000 - 90,000	18,200	48,500	53,400	62,500	72,900
€90,000 - 100,000	4,300	12,600	13,900	16,500	19,400
€100,000 - 150,000	8,700	21,600	24,400	29,800	36,400
€150,000 - 200,000	2,600	5,300	5,800	6,800	8,100
€200,000 - 500,000	2,500	4,600	5,000	5,800	6,700
€500,000 - 1,000,000	300	500	600	600	700
Over €1,000,000	100	200	200	300	300
Total in Employment	1,582,000	1,678,000	1,716,900	1,774,500	1,813,800

Figure 1.5 The Irish Salary Five Year Surge

These figures are phenomenal by any international standard at any time in history. These are the figures of a country – Ireland – who has *crossed the rubicon* during the last decade. No wonder wealth has increased in Ireland by 350% over 10 years. An interesting contrast could be to view the same figures for 1990 and 1995.

The third level of wealthy people are the **Ultra Wealthy**. Many of the ultra wealthy are 'old gold' or family empires and fall into the €26 million plus category. Concerns about creating and protecting their wealth are replaced by challenges around transferring their wealth to the next generation and legacy-building. Many quietly 'give back' in fundraising and philanthropy. The romantic notion of being able to live like a millionaire – quitting work and living off your wealth – is probably not realistic unless you have about €8 million in the bank. To maintain your spending – say €250,000 per annum – and protecting your assets against inflation and setbacks, a return of about 6-8 percent would be required on assets of €8 million. To be able to spend €250,000 a year without drawing a salary you would need to generate about €500,000 off your assets. That is, a three percent return would cover your spending habits while another three percent would be needed to protect your assets from inflation. Add another 2-3 percent as a safety measure. There are no fixed rules, of course, when it comes to a formula for drawing down money from your assets.

The two richest men in the world are Bill Gates of Microsoft, worth $60 billion and Warren Buffet worth $50 billion. These are extraordinary men and beyond the comprehension of even ordinary billionaires. Both are working hard to give away at least 50% of their fortunes. Sam Walton, one of the richest men on earth once said "There will come a time when big opportunities will be presented to you; when they do you must be in a position to take advantage of them". If you want to benchmark yourself against the men and women in this league, read the Fortune 500 and Sunday Times Rich List.

iv. Five Pathways To Becoming Wealthy

Wealthy men and women come in all kinds of classes and earn their wealth in many different ways as we have seen. But how do they earn their wealth? Today 85 percent of wealthy people are self-made, first generation, millionaires (the other 15 percent inherit their wealth) and all the indicators suggest that there are five pathways to becoming wealthy as follows:

1. Business Owners: The ability to start and build your own business – entrepreneurship – accounts for 74 percent of all self-made millionaires. In Ireland, about 20,000 new enterprises are started each year and there are about 200,000 business owners at any one time in the country. The casualty rate is high with 58 percent of start-ups failing within five years yet more than half the population dream about setting up their own business. In America, there are more than one million new business enterprises each year

CROSSING THE RUBICON: Seven Steps To Writing Your Own Personal Strategy

and the failure rate for start-ups is estimated as high as 80 percent. Across the EU the failure rate is 44 percent. Managerial incompetence and inexperience is the number one reason for business failure. Trying to have the lifestyle of your previous boss too early, while starving the business of funds to grow with the wrong kind of overhead are classic mistakes. Interestingly, the average self-made millionaire has been broke or nearly broke 2.4 times before becoming wealthy.

2. Corporate Managers: Being a highly paid executive in a fast-growth or very successful company is another way to get rich. About 10 percent of HNWIs get wealthy by being well paid and promoted as professional managers, earning stock options, bonuses and getting involved in profit sharing schemes. Ireland is well endowed with multi-national organisations that produce wealthy individuals.

Obviously bigger economies with huge corporations provide the scale and opportunity to produce millionaires from the management platform more readily. If you are consistently earning a remuneration package of several hundred thousand euros plus share options it is easier to see how they can join the HNWIs, provided you invest prudently of course.

3. The Professionals: About 10 percent of self-made millionaires are doctors, dentists, lawyers, architects, engineers, consultants and others with specialist degrees that can charge high fees for their services. These professionals' academic or specialised knowledge makes their contribution extremely valuable and their clients pay above the norm for their high value services.

They get paid more for what they have done – services rendered and their expertise – than for what they do in any specific transaction. According to the Competition Authority in Ireland, the average income of a senior council is €270,000 while the top 10 percent earn more than €600,000 a year.

4. The Creative Class: New professional roles, largely born out of the technology industry, are the creative class such as programmers and computer 'geeks'. These make up about five percent of self-made millionaires. Sales professionals, for example, in traditional roles never started their own business or earned professional degrees, but became very good at selling a product and are well paid for doing it. Selling is the oldest

profession and can be the vital talent for large and small businesses everywhere.

These professionals manage their money very smartly, investing it intelligently and making it grow until they become millionaires. Some sales executives earn huge bonuses and commissions because they create value in the sales process and deliver exceptional sales growth, one of the most important ingredients in business success. Others such as house designers, artists, professional writers – Cecilia Ahern, Jamie Oliver, John Rocha – are the more popularly known members of the creative class.

5. The One Percent Rest: The final category of self-made millionaires fall into the general category of entertainers, sports stars, authors, lottery winners and all other sources. These get lots of media attention but merely make up the numbers in real wealth terms. They are the exceptions to the rule in almost all cases for their category. For example, film stars make millions, but 95 percent of all actors earn very average incomes. Sports stars get lots of news, but most full-time sports professionals just about survive.

Roy Keane, the former Ireland and Manchester United football captain, earned about £80,000 per week with net assets of £40 million. The richest soccer player in 2005, David Beckham, topped the players rich list with assets of £110 million. The average salary for a premiership footballer in England is €973,000. Padraig Harrington, professional golfer, earns more than €4 million per year.

Bono and the U2 band are Ireland's richest entertainers with a fortune of €700 million through their musical ability and financial astuteness. Michael Flatley of 'Riverdance' and 'Lord of the Dance' fame is worth €550 million.

v. Five Value Drivers To Creating Wealth

What sort of activities do the four or five percent wealthy proportion of our population engage in that enables them to accumulate so much more wealth than the other 95 percent? And remember, 80 percent of wealthy people are first generation – in their own lifetime – self-made millionaires. We have explored the five pathways to becoming wealthy. Now let us explore the five underlying reasons why so few people get wealthy and the great majority of people stay financially poor:

i. Passion And Focus vs No Consideration Given To Being Wealthy

A burning desire and deep determination, which becomes a clearly focused passion, seems to be the number one differentiator in the journey to being a self-made millionaire and a high net worth individual. Entrepreneurs and professionals alike fuel this passion into developing a high level of specialised knowledge in their particular field. Whether it is the entrepreneurial intelligence of a business owner or the specialised expertise of a dentist, it makes their contribution more valuable and, consequently, more and more people are prepared to buy their product or pay them higher fees for this level of expertise. Their overall attitude seems to be to get good at what they love to do, then to get better, then to be the best in their field.

Successful entrepreneurs, for example, know their product inside out. They become an authority in their field. They specialise in those high-valued activities that are of greatest importance and then delight their customers with personalised and top-drawer attention. They realise that 20 percent of their activities generate 80 percent of their overall results and their ability to focus on critical success factors is a core competency in itself. They go the extra mile. They focus on their passion not their pension. They always do more than they are paid for. Their commitment and passion energises everyone around them. Their 'magnificent obsession' in the one or two drivers of their business – such as selling – compensates for all their neglected functions or personal weaknesses.

Let's look at the flip side of this equation. The majority of people who stay in the poor category lack focus, concentration and self-belief. All belief is eventually self-belief. Belief in a product or a cause or venture. The concept of adding-value to a product or doing more than they are paid for is a concept they may not fully embrace.

Being wealthy, in fact, is just not within their comprehension. They simply give it no meaningful consideration. In most cases, it simply never occurs to them that the road to being in the top 5-10 percent of income earners is possible and that the degree of hard work and relentless dedication is not that much different from treading the road most travelled. 'The time is going to pass anyway' is not a concept that is fully appreciated and, therefore, it gets little or no preparation or planning time. Planning for the 'long-haul' is always overtaken by the here and now. So what steps can you start to take – if you need to – to create financial mastery?

First, set a goal to get out of debt immediately. If you have a hand-to-mouth attitude, a 'rob Peter to pay Paul' mind-set, you must stop it immediately.

Sit down with a blank sheet of paper and ask yourself 'Why do I have such a shortfall? Why am I struggling?' It's critical that you think on paper about your finances. In other words, write it all down. Addition and subtraction tell the real truth about your current situation.

There are two sources of money mismanagement. One is spending your money too freely when you are doing well, and the other is borrowing when you are overextended. If you have accumulated debts, go to your creditors and work out a plan to pay them off over a period of time. Do some 'horse-trading'. Get out of the clutches of moneylenders. Even if you're broke, you don't have to act like you are poor. Set a plan to pay off your debts over time.

Second, stop buying on credit. Pay cash or do without that product. Perform plastic surgery on your credit cards. If you can't afford something, don't buy it. If you're in a financial mess, get rid of all your credit cards (bar one at most). Start this financial mastery process immediately. Then continue what you've started. This is not as easy as it looks. How many ventures have you started and not continued? Dozens? Probably. A resource based view of strategy is all about getting to grips with money because money is always a scarce resource and is a good score card for how you are doing in terms of overall success.

Third, consider yourself as a personal profit centre. You must set financial independence as one of your major goals, not just for the money but to be free to concentrate on higher order goals and strategies. You must think of yourself as a profit centre and establish some ratios and measures for your personal affairs. Here are some basics to start the financial mastery journey:

- Review All Your Insurance Policies: Get several independent assessments. Plug the gaps. How you structure your various insurances from life cover to mortgage protection is critically important. Protect yourself at all costs.

- Get Rid Of Your Personal Banking Overdraft: Your goal should be to live within your means and totally eliminate personal bank charges.

- Do You Have A Pension?: Is it adequately funded? Can you maximise your tax relief by making additional voluntary contributions? Only 25 percent of self-employed people have pensions and only 50 percent of the working population. Thinking long-term is the essence of strategy.

- Are You Claiming All Your Tax Reliefs?: Millions of euros in reliefs are unclaimed each year. Get a good tax advisor. Whether you are an employee, self-employed, business owner or investor you probably have scope to legitimately save money on your taxes.

ii. Financial Literacy vs A Poverty Consciousness

Wealthy men and women develop a prosperity consciousness quite early on in their lives. This leads to an appreciation of money in a different way. They realise that *it takes money to make money*, and that real wealth is generated from various cash sources. Passive income streams and residual incomes, of course, need seed capital to get them started. Through this awareness, they come to realise that there are three forms of income:

- Earned income generated by the sweat of your brow and where you work for money
- Passive income is where you leverage your resources – especially money – to work for you
- Portfolio income is derived from paper assets such as stocks and bonds.
- The kick-start to creating wealth is to transfer earned income into passive and portfolio income as early as possible. Making your money work passively for you is boosted by the tax system where earned income is levied very high and the capital gains on passive investments is levied at a lower rate.

Wealthy individuals come to realise the power of leveraging time, reputation, people, knowledge, service and the concept of adding-value. Learning to leverage money is the key to creating wealth. At its simplest, becoming wealthy is a function of earning enough money and learning to keep it and then putting some of it to work to make more money. In other words, your financial freedom as a rubicon strategist is anchored on the principle of leveraging earned income into passive income streams.

Learning the financial knowledge to build assets that buy other assets is an imperative. The vital distinction between building a career and building an asset bank is this: *What* you know is important to earn a living, *who* you get to know is vital to get wealthy. Too many corporate executives, for example, focus on status symbols and demonstrating how much they know, rather than financial literacy.

Financial literacy, in the first instance, involves very basic financial management. The starting point of all riches is based on the degree of discipline that you have to save money on a regular basis. It means getting out of debt and staying out of debt on everyday items except – perhaps – your house mortgage and car repayments. It starts with having the foresight to build a cash reserve so that you are ready to invest when an appropriate opportunity emerges.

Could you live on 90 percent of your present net income? Of course you could. That means you could save 10 percent. This discipline starts the game of wealth creation. The discipline of saving money builds confidence and character. You feel like you are taking control of your own destiny. Having money in the bank actually empowers you like nothing else.

So why does the average, hard working, well intentioned citizen never get wealthy? The primary reasons are because they never make a *clear and definite decision* to 'get serious' about building up their assets, saving a small proportion of their income each month or staying out of debt. Fear of failure is the number one reason that stops people reaching their full potential in life. The fear of success is closely related and literally blocks people from even thinking about the possibility of becoming a millionaire in their lifetime.

Ironically, becoming a millionaire in your lifetime is relatively simple for most people if they could realise the importance of the eighth wonder of the world, which is the miracle of compound interest. Albert Einstein called it "The greatest power in the universe". Look at it like this: If a 21 year old was to save €100 per month, from the age of 21 to 65, assuming a 10 percent compound growth, that is over the 44 working years of their worklife, they would be an automatic millionaire. If you were to stop smoking cigarettes you could save about €3,000 per year. Can you imagine the compound interest benefits of this over just one decade?

Keep in mind that the average millionaire is 48 before reaching their goal. But they believe they can do it from their 20s. The majority of wealthy people make progress slowly. They get wealthy over a long period of careful and incremental growth as a result of compound interest. People who struggle financially believe they cannot entertain such ideas and set out to prove themselves right by spending all they earn and more on everyday items. 'Spend less than you make' is financial advice that can literally transform your financial life.

iii. The Power Of Networking vs The Disease Of Procrastinating

Turning *who you know* into a valuable social capital can save you years of hard work. Networking is a form of leverage that has a multiplier effect. Networking is the process of creating and developing contacts for mutual benefit. Knowing the right people and being known by them could literally change the course of your life. Learning to expand your list of contacts and expanding your social network is something successful people do as a matter of course. Successful people make it their business to attend functions and join the associations that like-minded people attend.

By joining your local chamber of commerce or attending conferences, exhibitions or evening events by your trade association you increase the probability of bumping into invited speakers, special guests or the movers and shakers in your industry.

Not only should you attend these kinds of events, you should volunteer to serve on the committee or get into a position of authority so you can leverage that position to add-value to your own position. Becoming actively involved in community organisations or a sports club, such as a golf club, are other excellent ways to become a master networker.

How do you stay poor? Network with the wrong people, at the wrong time, in the wrong place. Putting off until tomorrow, that which can be done today, is a major cause of inefficiency and entering the trap of poverty consciousness. In 1927, Don Marquis wrote that "Procrastination is the art of keeping up with yesterday". Procrastination on something as simple as building your base of contacts or opening a savings deposit account, can prevent you from becoming wealthy. Procrastination is the theft of time and of life. Procrastination keeps you poor.

iv. Communicator Extraordinaire vs The Pleasure Principle

You are in the business of communication, no matter what need you fill or industry you ply your trade in. Successful men and women have developed extraordinary talent in at least one primary area of communication. For example, they could be excellent at performing in a meeting, or in face-to-face negotiation encounters, or at influencing customers with their enthusiasm, or at making a presentation to a group, or with the written word. Virtually every entrepreneur, for example, is excellent in the art and science of selling. Their ability to persuade, influence or negotiate a deal with a multitude of stakeholders – suppliers, staff, customers, professionals – is one of the secrets of their success. It is no surprise that entrepreneurs form the biggest category of wealthy people. Their levels of entrepreneurial intelligence, fuelled by their self-belief and passion for their cause or belief in their product, makes them virtually unstoppable. Selling is a transfer of enthusiasm. That's why entrepreneurs are nearly always the number one sales generator in their own company. However, sales oriented people can be bad managers/owners as they look too much at the future sales potential over the present financial position.

The vast majority of people – about 80 percent – retire poor, because of what economists call their inability to delay gratification. The average person has an irresistible compulsion to spend almost every cent they make and whatever else they can borrow or buy on credit. The ability to refrain from spending everything you make is a fundamental principle of becoming wealthy. The great psychologist Sigmund Freud called it the pleasure principle. He said all human action is driven by two motivators, the desire for gain (the need to move towards gain or pleasure) and the fear of loss (the need to move away from discomfort or pain). In our modern society children are conditioned to associate spending money with pleasure and enjoyment and associate saving money with pain and discomfort. This mental conditioning determines our attitudes as adults towards financial literacy and is the underlying reason for financial failure and poverty later in life.

Keep in mind that the average self-made millionaire has been broke or nearly broke 2.4 times. And that it takes the average self-made millionaire 22 years to reach their goal according to the authors of *The Millionaire Next Door*. A millionaire mentor once advised me "Making your first million is extremely difficult, but the second and subsequent millions are almost inevitable".

This is because you have embraced the discipline and habits to take the necessary actions. These habits change *who you are* – your character – and *what you do*, forever. Even if you lose all your money, through some misfortune, you will make it back again because you have learned the millionaire code. This success template – this code – becomes a framework for all your other endeavours!

The Village Blacksmith in the poem "Looked the whole world in the face, for he owed not any man". That was a long time ago! Today debt is as much part of life as taxes and change. The Central Bank in Ireland reports that our total borrowings now exceed our annual income but draw some comfort from the fact that 82 percent is asset backed mortgages. Debt is debt is debt and robbing Peter to pay Paul through credit card shuffling is a vicious circle that most people never break free from.

Debt, of course, can be positive or negative. When you borrow for an activity that gives a higher return than the cost of the debt it is positive. Higher income groups borrow more to buy appreciating assets especially when interest rates are low. Debt is relatively cheaper for the rich as it is risk-adjusted – they can more easily tighten their belts.

You must break this cycle of subconscious programming with regard to spending and saving. You must discipline yourself to realise that if you are hard on yourself now, life will be easy on you in the longer term.

v. Long Term Perspective vs Immediate Gratification

Long term perspective – the fifth reason for financial success – is your ability to project into the future, when considering the implications of day-to-day planning and deciding on important life choices. This seems to be central to financial independence. The majority of long term wealth is 'slow money', carefully invested and well thought out.

Medical students, for example, need a 10-15 year perspective to be a surgeon. They earn the right to prestige, status and a high standard of living through years of sacrifice and delayed gratification. Those 10-15 years of study and work is an investment in their career for the rest of their lives. Savings and planning for the future is long-term perspective in action. A young couple putting €50 a month into an education plan for their newborn child is a couple with long term perspective. They are willing to sacrifice in the short term to assure better results and outcomes in the long term. The average millionaire spends 20-30 hours per month working on their finances and learning about investment opportunities. The average person spends 2-3 hours per month working on money matters and that's usually at bill paying time.

How far you can project your thinking into the future when deciding upon what you are going to do or not do in 'the present moment' is the single most important predictor of long term success. Entrepreneurs, for example, rarely consider an immediate payback. And they regard short term sacrifice as part and parcel of their wealth creation. In other words, they have developed the ability to delay gratification by focusing on their long term vision and financial payback.

Earning money is only the first step in wealth creation, holding on to it and making it work for you is the second step. It's how much you keep that is the bedrock of financial success. Every deposit in a savings account adds up and provides the seed capital if an opportunity should arise, such as to invest in a property or take a share in a business which would allow you to generate passive cash flow. This is that passive or residual income stream again!

For many people *crossing the rubicon* means 'getting serious about their financial affairs'. The principles of financial success are eternal. In the first instance you should develop a very clear understanding that achieving financial independence in the first instance is more a psychological discipline than any other factor. Fortunately or unfortunately, it is the primary medium by which worldly success is measured. Set a goal therefore to read six to ten books on the psychology and techniques of money management just to stay abreast of the mechanics of modern-day money management. Money markets are volatile. Even the experts are struggling to keep up as politics, economics and even individual idiosyncrasies can rock the global economy. So, as you reflect on your current situation and write your personal strategy, consider the five drivers of wealth creation:

- Plug into your passion and channel this self-belief into getting exceptionally good at *what you do*. Then, just do it.
- Decide to single-mindedly focus on becoming wealthy. Learn how. Take the long road.
- Learn to network. Take massive and immediate action at all times. Never procrastinate.
- Discipline yourself to live well below your means and be prepared to make huge sacrifices of time and forego the social niceties of life in the short term.
- Engage in long term perspective. Think and act 5, 10 and 20 years into the future. Everything adds up over time. Get wealthy slowly.

Wealthy people learn to add-value to the life or work of other people. Adding-value and constantly striving to do things better, faster, cheaper, easier is the key to wealth creation. Making money is a basic competency but it takes hard work, discipline, knowledge and practice. But since the vast majority of wealthy people are *self-made* it is obviously a learnable skill.

1.6 TIME AND LIFE MANAGEMENT ... HOW DO YOU USE TIME?

Patrick Kavanagh, the great Irish playwright, said "Time has its own part to play". How true this is with regard to your personal strategy. The essence of time was beautifully captured by Norman McLean in *A River Runs Through It* as follows: "Poets talk about 'spots of time', but it is really fishermen who experience eternity compressed into a moment. No one can tell what a spot of time is until suddenly the whole world is a fish and the fish is gone. I shall remember that son of a bitch forever". Time is life.

Here are eight great questions that you should consider as part of your personal strategy review. The single most powerful and immediate impact you can make towards *crossing the rubicon* is in this time management arena:

i. ARE YOU BEING REACTIVE OR PROACTIVE?

The 80/20 rule – the Pareto principle – tells us that 20 percent of the input into any process commonly generates 80 percent of the output. For example, 20 percent of your customers may account for 80 percent of your total business turnover. Or 20 percent of your product lines may account for 80 percent of your total sales.

It follows that 20 percent of the time you spend on your Key Result Areas (KRAs) produces 80 percent of your results. When and how you use this 20 percent is obviously vitally important. By examining a cause-and-effect situation, you can isolate key factors for remedial action. In other words, by identifying 'the vital few' (the 20 percent) over the 'trivial many' (the 80 percent) you can find the secret to your long-term success and improvement. Be careful of reactive management.

A production manager explained to me that his company had comprehensive information on absenteeism but management had never sat down and analysed who were the main absentees or the potential causes of absenteeism in their business. He reacted to the situation as it arose and somehow, always sorted out the gaps in his production scheduling. Because he had the information on-hand, he spent several hours analysing the absenteeism of the previous year. He found that 22 percent of his staff (absentees) accounted for 84 percent of all lost time. He decided to be proactive with this information!

When he analysed it further through discussion with his supervisors and staff he found that the major cause was a group of young mothers who had difficulty finding babysitters to look after their young babies. In the end, the solution was simple. He financed the building of a crèche in an old office within the factory. Over the following six months, the absentee rate dropped by 70 percent.

Further examples of the 80/20 rule can be seen in other aspects of industry and business. We know from training sales people across a wide range of industries that sales representatives spend only about 20 percent of their time in front of their customers.

More than 80 percent of time is spent in the office, travelling or wasting time. Sales representatives who just increase time in front of the customer (selling face-to-face) by five percent or 10 percent may be doing enough to make a significant bottom line difference to sales. Most sales representatives have never analysed their time in this regard. Most of their managers have not done so either.

Your application of the Pareto discipline to your time management, to proactively mark out time to achieve important tasks and goals, is critical to success. Doing the wrong thing very well is the height of folly. Think about your reactiveness as you review your current situation and prepare to change *what you do* in your goal setting exercise. Creative abandonment means you must stop doing certain things in order to find the time to do other things. Writing your personal strategy is a KRA, a 20 percent proactive project. But you must give it the time.

ii. ARE YOU EFFICIENT OR EFFECTIVE?

A constant challenge for you is your ability to maximise your personal productivity. The key to conquering this challenge is understanding and mastering the difference between effectiveness and efficiency. Being *efficient* means doing the job *right*, whereas being *effective* means doing the *right* job right. There is an enormous difference between the two. But it's a subjective judgment call in many cases. Only you can decide.

Most people are so busy cutting wood that they don't take the time to sit down and sharpen the axe. Just hitting harder and going faster doesn't necessarily mean you're more effective. Confusing *busyness* with *business* is a major blind spot for many people.

The efficient manager, for example, gets involved in everything. He is obsessed with making an impression: 'Look at how busy I am and how hard I work.' He suffers from the 'martyr' syndrome. The effective manager concentrates on KRAs – the 20 percent important, vital, few tasks. Focusing on these tasks moves you to a fundamentally better position in overall strategic terms. So, one of the most important questions you should continually ask yourself is: 'Am I efficient or am I effective?'

A key executive in a client organisation just couldn't find the time to complete his KRAs. Together we analysed his time management and identified four critical activities that he needed to change. For example, he travelled 28,000 business miles the previous year in his motor car. In his reactive mode, he felt his job was to 'jump in the car' to solve every problem.

Calculating that he travelled at about 40 mph in the city, he spent about 700 hours or the equivalent of 17 work-weeks in his car – that's like driving non-stop from January to May. He was astonished with this information and its implications and set about reorganising his journeys. He cut them down to 14,000 miles. This change alone gifted him 350 hours to proactively focus on the 20 percent KRAs that he had been neglecting.

iii. DO YOU CONCENTRATE ON URGENT TASKS OR IMPORTANT TASKS?

In your current situation assessment you start to identify, through your strategic thinking and planning process, the important success areas of your personal life, career and business. You start to see the wood from the trees. You understand the importance of saying 'No'. You know how to lock yourself away for hours or even days of concentrated thinking and planning time. As a strategist, as opposed to an operational person, you do this every week and may feel cheated if you have not scheduled a certain portion of your week to important long-term strategic and vision-related activities.

An important task is a high-benefit task. An urgent task is time-bounded – if you don't do it by a certain time, the benefit of doing it will be lost or reduced. Watch out for the urgent task crowding out the important task. Schedule time for the important jobs during your personal best time.

RUBICON STEP 1: Current Situation Analysis

Making important decisions requires a long-term thinking perspective that helps you to justify some things you need to do in the short term and guides you away from things you should not do. Your big decisions are often high in importance and low in urgency. Focus on the decisions that are directly related to your goals and strategies.

A manager, who completed a comprehensive three month-long analysis of her time, told me that 18 percent of her incoming telephone callers took up 74 percent of her total telephone time. This startled her. She immediately set in motion ways and means to do business in a different and more concise way with these callers. She was reactive to every call and far too available. She proactively set about educating the telephone offenders and changed the situation over the following six weeks.

Ask yourself the twin questions: 'Am I being efficient?' or 'Am I being effective?' and 'Do I concentrate on urgent tasks or important tasks?' – at regular times every day. You will have great difficulty with honestly answering these questions for yourself if you are unfocused and have no clear personal strategy.

It will cause you great stress and turmoil if you are confused about the words 'effective/efficient', 'proactive/reactive' and 'important/urgent'. The key to personal leadership and top performance is clear purposeful action on the important, effective tasks that you choose to proactively work on. Coincidentally, it's also the cure for stress and other illnesses.

iv. WHAT IS THE MOST VALUABLE USE OF YOUR TIME RIGHT NOW?

To answer this question fully, you must consider the power of purpose. What is your overall purpose? Why do you get up in the morning? What motivates you? Are you going through the motions or are you living out your dreams? What is your calling? Where do you fit? What difference are you making to other people's lives? What are your expectations?

Crossing the rubicon is the psychological act of 'getting serious' about your life more than anything and, above all, it needs dedicated time and due attention. 'What is the most valuable use of my time this minute, this hour, this day, this week, this month, this year' helps bring clarity and focus to your current situation more than any other question in resource management. Lack of clarity and diffusion of effort are the twin saboteurs of success. Purposeful action is its antidote.

Henry Van Dyke probably sums up time best in 1905 when he wrote "Time is too slow for those who wait, too swift for those who fear, too long for those who grieve, too short for those who rejoice; But for those who love, Time is eternity."

v. WHAT ARE YOU DOING TODAY TO ACHIEVE YOUR LONG-TERM STRATEGY?

If you don't know where you're going, there is no doubt but that you will end up somewhere. What are you doing today to move you closer to achievement of your goals?

The secret of this strategy process is not that you end up somewhere, even if it is a better place than before, but that you end up at the place that you set out to end up. Please don't fool yourself. If your strategy is not written down, it's not strategy; it's a nice idea. In formulating your strategy, a step in any direction will not do. You must ensure that each step is in the right direction.

Your mind is capable of storing thousands and thousands of facts and ideas, but it can only focus on those important things that you are reminded of on a continual basis. It is not possible to be <u>proactive</u> and focused clearly on <u>the important</u> and <u>the effective</u> without beating away the other thousands of trivial pieces of information and demands on your time.

Long-term perspective is the ability to project into the future when considering the implications of day-to-day planning and deciding upon important personal strategy life-choices. This ability is critical to your strategic success.

Immediate gratification and short term thinking is a major reason for poverty and consequent unhappiness. The average manual labourer, for example, has no bank account, let alone a savings plan and refuses to consider the option of saving 10 percent of their income as an investment in their future prosperity.

Learning to save is a mental discipline. Learning to live on 90 percent of your income is well within the reach of the vast majority of the population, yet the vast majority of people are not prepared to make the short term, minor sacrifice, for the long term beneficial effects. The great tragedy is that the time is going to pass anyway, the only question is how much will you be worth in 10, 20, 30 years time? Of course, long term perspective also improves short term decision making.

vi. WHAT MAKES YOU PRODUCTIVE?

To help you answer this question, draw a 360 degree blank circle and start to divide it into sections regarding the key accountabilities of your job. How much long-term thinking time have you allocated in there? You must allocate 'strategy time' and slice it into your scheduling and planning system.

What is your mission? What are your strategic goals? Focus and clarity are key competencies for your success. You cannot honestly answer the 'What makes me productive?' question unless you are clear and totally focused on your major definite purpose and your vision for the future (rubicon steps 4 & 5).

I speak to thousands of managers each year at public and in-house meetings and seminars and I ask them "What's your single biggest daily and ongoing challenge?" Their answers are invariably 'overloaded', 'too busy', and 'not enough time in the day'. Many of these managers are very efficient, reactive people but they are not effective and proactive. You must discipline yourself to be proactive, effective and productive on your 20 percent important tasks.

vii. WHAT CAN YOU, AND ONLY YOU, DO?

Your ability to concentrate and focus on one or two KRAs that only you can complete will set you apart from everyone else in terms of bottom line results. Become a deadline person. Become a completion person.

Commitment to the closure of a task by a set date takes courage. If these tasks are transformational in nature and you make it a habit to deadline them you will achieve more in 60 days than an ordinary person will achieve in a year.

What are your primary responsibilities at home? At work? In other words, have you established what your own KRAs are?

During my talks and seminars, I ask managers to engage in a practical exercise to demonstrate my 'zoom in/zoom out' focus technique. I ask them to hold their index finger about 18 inches in front of their face and to focus all their attention on that finger. They can clearly see their fingerprint lines. I then ask them to become aware that everything in the background and on the horizon is blurred and unclear. I then ask them to zoom out like a wide-angle zoom lens of a camera and bring the distant horizon and background into full view.

They still keep their finger in place but are now aware that it is quite difficult to zoom in on the finger and keep a crystal clear picture of the background. Move your finger a few inches from left to right in front of your face to demonstrate the need to adjust and be flexible in moving towards the big picture.

You will have figured out the purpose of the exercise by now. It is the ability to zoom in on short and medium term requirements while at the same time having the ability to focus on the wider horizon and bring it into crystal clear vision at a moment's notice.

You must be able to align the short-term projects with the medium term projects and with your big picture vision. Alignment is a word that all great strategists understand. Focus is another. Closure on KRAs is another.

viii. WHAT WOULD YOU DO DIFFERENTLY?

The eighth and final question is a zero-based question. Zero-based questions help you to make up your mind about critical issues and therefore save enormous amounts of wasted time, stress and people problems. Apply a zero-based question as follows: 'Knowing what I now know about this person that I have hired, or this situation that I've got into, or this product that's not selling, would I still get involved with it again?' If the answer is 'no', you need to decide to either rectify the situation or get out of it. Learn to terminate situations that are on the slippery slope to nowhere.

I have personally made numerous mistakes in hoping that the people I have hired or have been associated with would work out. When a relationship goes negative it's very difficult, and often impossible, to bring it back to positive.

You should never wrestle with a pig because both of you get dirty, but the pig likes it! Be careful about getting into long drawn-out tangles with the people that are not in line with your strategic thinking and planning. Finish the relationship. It's best for you and probably for the other person.

Implement these actions with focus and determination and your life will change very quickly. When something needs to be done, take decisive and immediate action to complete it. This will mark you out more than any other productivity factor. Procrastination and 'the slow no' is not for you. Develop a sense of urgency and a reputation for speed and dependability.

1.7 MASTERING THE CHALLENGES OF CHANGE ... WHAT CHOICES HAVE YOU?

Change is the only constant today. But change itself has changed. There has always been change, but now it's faster, accelerated, even exponential. How you assimilate change into your life is very important. Gandhi wrote that we should "Be the change that you want in the world." In other words "Each one, change one". Becoming different is the essence of change, but this 'becoming different' can take many forms from a wide scope to a narrow scope, and from having a high impact across your total life to a low impact.

These two variables — scope and impact — can be presented as a 2 x 2 matrix which forms four quadrants or approaches to change. This thinking framework may help you to see change in a more strategic way. Review the four quadrants of change in the diagram below:

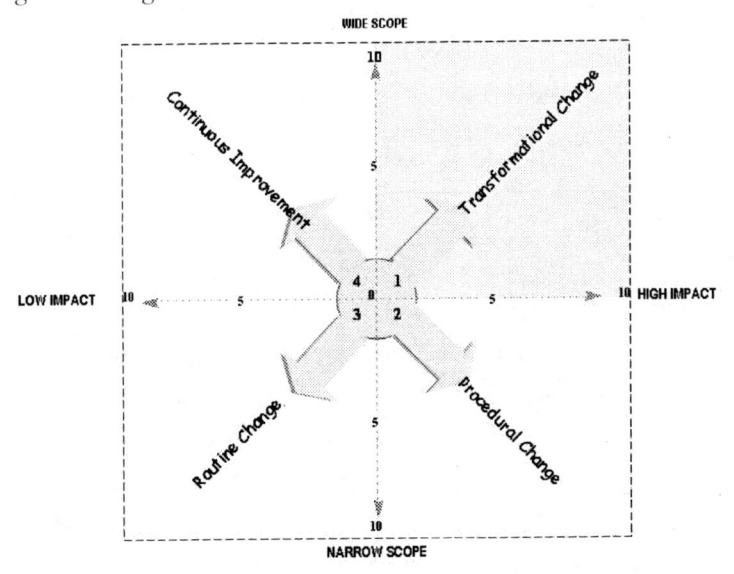

Figure 1.7 Four Change Options: The Scope and Impact of Change

i. Transformational Change: Wide Scope, High Impact

Change that takes a wide scope with high impact can totally change the way you live your life. It is macro change and requires a total rethink about your positioning, how you deploy your talents, your networking and time priorities. This kind of change is transformational and important, but usually not urgent. It requires a major rethink about 'how you do things' in your life. Most people have difficulty in identifying where and how to begin a change process of this nature.

In business, major resistance may occur unless the rationale for such sweeping change is communicated through several channels and, over time, to everybody in the organisation. Globalisation, fierce competition and technological innovations drives this kind of change.

Such business changes could include re-engineering, major restructuring, downsizing or strategic innovation. A move from traditional line management to a project or self-directed work team model could be an example of total strategic innovation. A merger with another company or an acquisition of a former competitor are other examples.

In professional life, it may not be unusual for you to have three or more transformational changes in your lifetime in this revolutionary world. Transformational change could be a change of career, moving from employment to self-employment or emigrating. Dealing with a sudden redundancy or termination of employment can set you back or set you up depending on how you deal with the change. You can become a victim or a master of change … either way it can be transformational.

In personal life, it could mean getting married, having a couple of children, or building that dream house. It could mean winning the lotto or gaining an inheritance. One man said his life was 'devastated' when his spouse died of cancer and left him to rear three children. A dynamic business owner sold his business and transformed his lifestyle when he got a 'tap on the shoulder' in the form of an early heart attack.

Procrastination and denial are classic reasons men and women do not make the fundamental changes necessary to reach their full potential. Ongoing stress is the best test that you are not deploying your talents to best advantage. Research indicates that half the population are in the wrong job. These may be factors for your consideration in the first quadrant.

ii. Procedural Change: High Impact, Narrow Scope

'Doing 100 things one percent better' can have more impact than 'doing one thing 100 percent better' is the basic premise of quadrant two. A micro change can have high impact over time. This inevitably means better management of the moments of impression and inter-relationships in your life. Small improvements consistently worked at, over time, can have a cumulative effect. Everything counts. Everything adds up.

'What kind of family would this family be if everyone around here did things just like me?' is a tough question for each member of a family to ask. If you first identified your own marginal 'areas for improvement' and concentrated on improving them, wouldn't this make a difference?

You undoubtedly have key tasks within your own area of control, which only you can identify. For many, personal change is perceived as unimportant and not very urgent, characterised by a mindset of 'I'm OK in my comfort zone'. Complacency sets in almost imperceptibly and eventually takes hold like a form of virus.

iii. Routine Change: Narrow Scope, Low Impact

A micro change with low impact is regular, routine and safe. Micro changes are basic maintenance initiatives. Such change is well within your comfort zone and part and parcel of everyday life.

At work, routine change may serve to regularise workflow or production procedures. It could be as simple as tidying up your desk and filing that pile or cleaning up your databank or having an image consultant give you the once-over regarding your dress code.

At home, routine change is the annual spring clean or building that conservatory out back or buying that hot tub as a leisure and health treatment for the family. Or it could mean going to your son or daughter's football game more often.

iv. Continuous Improvement: Low Impact, Wide Scope

In the world of work, performance improvement initiatives such as a total quality process, the installation of ISO 9000 standards and the development of self-directed work teams have been carried out on a macro scale in many organisations but with, in general, low impact. Some organisations benefited from them but most initiatives have had a low net impact effect on companies.

Continuous macro changes, however, are necessary improvement interventions. Above all they bring concentration and collective focus to bear on creating personal or business advantage. At home or in work, humans have a natural tendency to be diverted or become sloppy because of the multitude of demands and many hats that they are expected to wear these days. So always be on the lookout for a better way not just for the improvement itself but for the focus it brings. Focus gives purpose and direction to your change process.

Personal development is an example of a change process that has an initial low impact but you can take a very wide scope on it. Getting to understand the 'chatterbox' in your head and the inner voices that talk to you can take a whole lifetime. Socrates said that to "Know thyself" was the biggest task and first responsibility of every well intentioned person. Another example is saving money and building up a savings account.

You are unlikely to embark on a change process unless you are being pushed into it - unless you are experiencing some form of pain, restlessness or dissatisfaction. On the other hand, you will need to be pulled towards improvement or some potential advantage.

You have two major motivators. On the negative side, it's the fear of loss (pain). On the positive side, it's the desire for gain. If these positive and negative factors are only of passive or academic interest to you, then significant personal (or organisational) change will probably not occur. Your job, on the one hand is to increase the desire for improvement and on the other hand to reduce the potential for discomfort or loss. Both efforts require lots of influencing. It's a push and pull approach.

"If the rate of change outside your organisation is greater than the rate of change inside your organisation then the end is in sight" are the immortal words of Jack Welsh, former CEO of GE. Apply this same sentiment to your own personal and professional situation. Are you a victim of change or in control of change. Change is, ultimately, 80 percent an inside job and only 20 percent circumstantial. Becoming different is change. Manage it.

1.8 TALENT ANALYSIS ... HOW DO YOU TURN YOUR TALENTS INTO COMPETENCIES?

Where have you the greatest potential for performance improvement and excellence in your current role? In which areas of your work do you show most flair? Where do your talents shine best? Where do you get your best results and sense of satisfaction? What do you love to do? When you can answer these questions, you have probably identified, in the broadest sense, some areas of talent for you. These are areas of work and life where you tend to excel and achieve superior performance levels.

Everybody has talents, but most people do not know what their talents are. When you ask them, they look at you with a 'blank stare' and respond in terms of subject knowledge. In other words, most people focus on what they do – "I am an accountant" – instead of identifying their talents and the supporting skills to achieve positive and successful results.

For an organisation, *Talent Management* can be defined as 'applying best practices in the identification, cultivation, recruitment and retention of a qualified, effective workforce'. It means the development of 'talent' as a strategic asset. By recruiting high performers and people with hard-to-replace skillsets, and ensuring that they are consistently made aware that their skills, time and talent is talent management in action. This can be achieved through creative compensation methods and a strong succession planning process that targets an employee for their next internal career step and how they can get there. This helps improve retention, overall productivity and this talent pool becomes your best referral source for other candidates who will become your next high performers and so the cycle goes on. Potential employees have become much more selective about choosing their jobs and those with strong skills find themselves in strong negotiating positions.

Your challenge is to become an 'employee of-choice' by doing a thorough talent assessment or an employer-of-choice if you are a business owner. An effective talent management system sets leaders apart from their competitors. Communicating a clear vision of the future to your staff contributes to higher retention, better productivity levels and a more profitable engagement all round.

For most people their talents are hiding in plain sight but, so interwoven, they can be hard to detect. However, they do leave tracks and can be identified, recognised and developed. More importantly, talent can be turned into competencies to deliver consistently excellent performance levels.

Competencies are the combination of behaviours, attitudes, values, skills learned practices and emotional intelligence applied by effective people to deliver superior results.

There are definite methodologies for identifying your talents and turning them into consistently excellent performance. This can be done by benchmarking, measuring and developing the critical competencies necessary for superior performance and results in any position in your company.

In order to develop those talents a bit more scientifically, we recommend you work on and develop the performance style that best matches your natural behaviours, your motivators or drivers and your underlying attributes. Then add skill, knowledge and experience to put the icing on the cake. Personal talent management is about turning the combination of these factors into competency strengths to deliver business results and personal transformation.

In the Strategic Human Performance Improvement (SHPI) model we take you through a systematic process as follows:

DEFINING
THE CORE
COMPETENCIES
OF THE JOB

MEASURING
YOUR PERSONAL &
PROFESSIONAL
TALENTS & COMPETENCIES

DEVELOPING
COMPETENCY SOLUTIONS TO HELP
DELIVER CONSISTENTLY
EXCELLENT PERFORMANCE

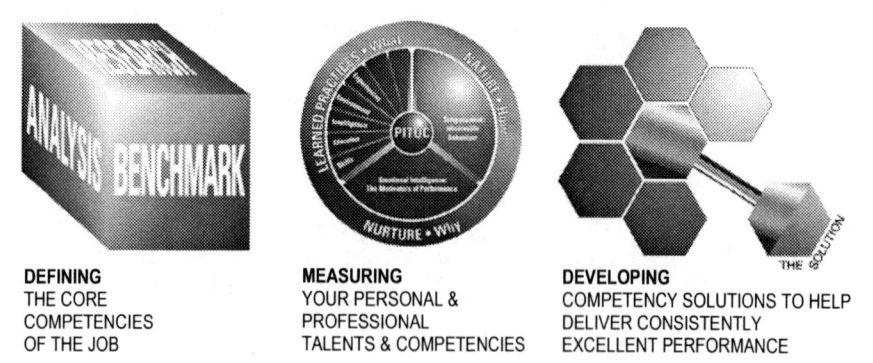

Figure 1.8a The Strategic Human Performance Improvement (SHPI) Model

First, *define* the job and critical benchmarks surrounding the position. Ask internal 'job experts' to comprehensively answer these questions: If this job could voice an opinion, what would it say are the talents and competencies necessary for superior performance? How do the key accountabilities, job description and job responsibilities set out the framework for defining the competencies of the job? In other words, look at your job first and identify the critical success factors necessary to make it a big success. Do this for your own job and for all jobs under your responsibility.

Second, *measure* the most important personal and professional competencies and benchmark them against the best-practice job definition. Research indicates that the source of 50 percent of job performance problems is that people are in the wrong job. Another 25 percent of on-the-job performance problems is the inability to identify the 'gaps' between the competencies of the person and the requirements of the job. The fit between the job and the person is vital to performance excellence.

Third, *develop and implement* appropriate solutions to bridge the competency gaps and align human performance interventions with the strategic thinking and planning of the business.

Talent identification management is a systems thinking methodology for organisations to attract, recruit, retain, identify and develop talent.

There are four steps in this process:

1. **Assessing Talent Pool Needs:** During this step, the capabilities of current members of the organisation has to be assessed, and the current and future competencies needed is gauged. The gap between the two (if any) is the new talent that is required.

2. **Spot Talent:** Individuals with leadership and/or management potential have to be identified, as well as Subject Matter Experts and key knowledge holders.

3. **Develop Talent:** Plans for developing talent within the organisation, either existing or acquired, must be established in order to prepare for future needs. As well, opportunities for job rotation should be identified, in order to expose talent to new experiences.

4. **Retain Talent:** Once a talent base has been created, it needs to be retained. In order to do so, recognition plans and reward schemes can be put into place.

TALENT MANAGEMENT: TWIN OBJECTIVES

There are two aspects to turning talents into effective competencies:
1. Developing the more functional, technical competencies, which are 'learned practice' during your career
2. Utilising your innate leadership 'being' competencies

How well you can deploy your natural talents and match them to the competencies of the job will greatly increase your levels of personal mastery and performance management.

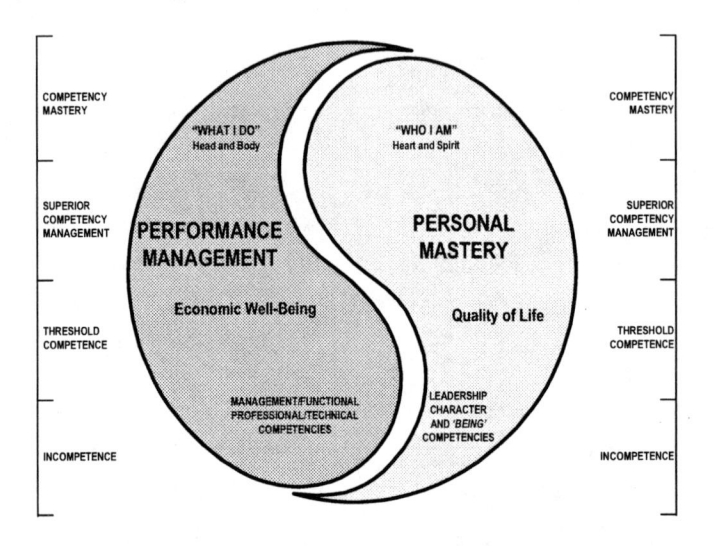

Figure 1.8b The Talent Management Model: Performance and Personal Mastery are two aspects of competency development

Talent Management requires a framework to identify where you need to 'get to work'. Most managers neglect the personal mastery side of the equation and suffer constant 'pain' in this area. The Talent Management model helps you determine where you stand on both dimensions.

A scale on both dimensions can help you see how you score, ranging from incompetence, to threshold competency (often regarded as entry level technical proficiency etc.), to superior competency mastery (the thrust of this programme), and higher levels of excellence and near perfect performance (mastery).

RUBICON STEP 1: Current Situation Analysis

TALENT MANAGEMENT: TASK & PROCESS FOCUS

Your willingness and ability to identify areas for improvement is the first step to all learning and improvement.

Talent Management can be sub-divided into identifiable areas to help on your competency development journey. Your talents are hiding in plain sight, but so interwoven that they are hard to detect. However, they do leave tracks and the clues are to be found somewhere within this talent model:

Teams
Feedback
Evaluation
Appraisal

Coaching
Mentoring
Personality
Advice
Customer
Rewardship
Leadership
Performance
Evaluation
Resources

Marketing
Productivity
Development

Interpersonal
Intelligencies
Career Management

Managing
Expectations
Performance
Career Plans
Reward Systems

"WHAT I DO"
Head and Body

Professional Competency
Mastery
Knowledge Management
The job
Performance Management
Financial Intelligence
Wealth Strategy
Business Acumen
HP1
Technical Strategic Insight
Customer Focus
Innovation

Professional Style
The Outer Experience

TASK FOCUS

"WHO I AM"
Heart and Spirit

Character Assessment
Emotional Intelligence
Natural Talents
Personal Competency Mastery
Personality Factor
Success Anchors: Happiness Index
Natural Principles of Life
Attitude Management
Personal Responsibility
Intrapersonal Intelligence
Learning to Change
Social Intelligence
Self-image Psychology
Personal Strategy

Image and Values
The Internal Game

PROCESS FOCUS

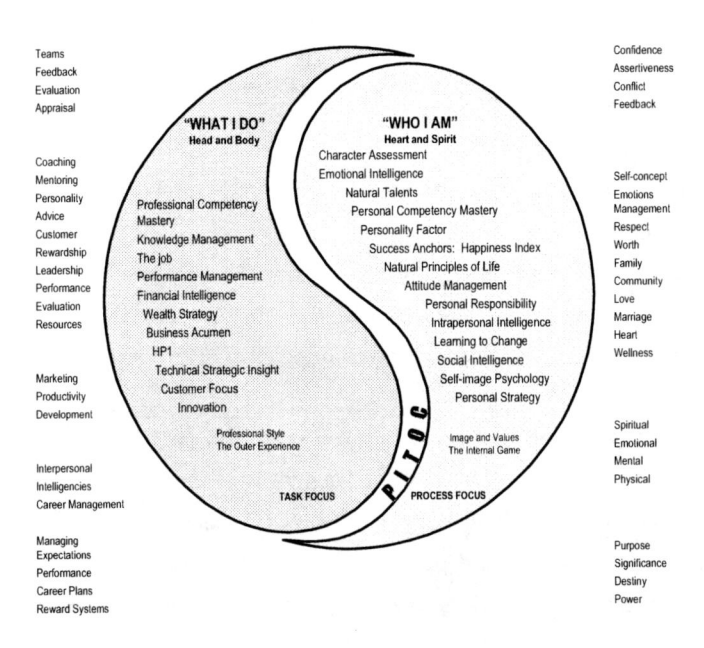

Confidence
Assertiveness
Conflict
Feedback

Self-concept
Emotions
Management
Respect
Worth
Family
Community
Love
Marriage
Heart
Wellness

Spiritual
Emotional
Mental
Physical

Purpose
Significance
Destiny
Power

Figure 1.8c The Talent Management Model: Combining
Talents Into Competency Strengths

"Most people do not know what their strengths are. When you ask them, they look at you with a blank stare, or they respond in terms of subject knowledge, which is the wrong answer" is how Peter Drucker described the journey to find your talents.

In summary, for an organisation, talent management is the process of recruiting, motivating and retaining the 'best and brightest' employees in order to enhance organisational effectiveness and achieve organisational goals.

For you, talent management is a leadership responsibility to identify and build on your natural qualities and innate abilities in certain fields of activity. Nelson Mandela's famous speech in 1994 sums it up nicely:

> *"Our deepest fear is not that we are inadequate.*
> *Our deepest fear is that we are powerful beyond measure.*
> *It is our light not our darkness, that most frightens us.*
> *And as we let our light shine,*
> *We unconsciously give other people permission to do the same"*

Many talents, like diamonds, come disguised as hard work. You must be prepared to confront interesting problems and challenges in order to avail of the opportunities that are hiding in your talents. The key method of handling problems is to address them when they are still small because they will probably not go away. Secondly, make a decision to bring closure to all outstanding issues.

A talent that is not mined, honed and developed has the same effect as a non existent talent. If you do not use your talents, they are of no benefit to you. Therefore, unless you identify your area of excellence, your hidden and expressed talents and you are prepared to take the necessary steps to move forward and utilise your talents, you will not achieve the enjoyment, job satisfaction and business results that is within your potential and talents.

It is important that you recognise and utilise your talents and gifts, lest you go to your grave with your music still in you. Enjoy your talents and enjoy exploring your potential in life and work and success will come your way.

1.9 PRODUCT/MARKET OVERVIEW ... DO YOU HAVE OPTIONS?

The *Product/Market Growth Matrix* is a classic business template that you can adapt to show the choices you may have open to you on your personal strategy journey. Consider your options. Keeping some alternatives in mind is always a good strategy. Moving from the original business growth dimension to personal/family and professional/career dimensions of your life is very evident in this exercise. Keep thinking 'as if' you are the self-employed CEO of your own personal services or marketing company.

Plotted together, on a four quadrant matrix, you can see where you are at present and where you could be.

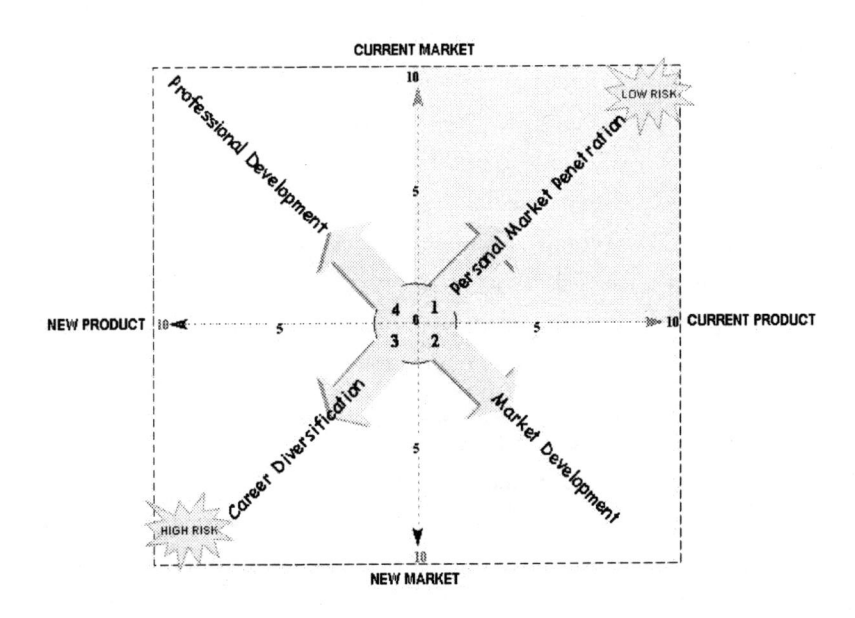

Figure 1.9 Product/Market Growth Matrix: Choices Open To You

At a commercial level, you are a product, offering a service or 'portfolio of solutions' to meet some need, just like a company. You are also in a marketplace selling your trade. In this classic marketing model, therefore, there are two variables to consider: you as a product and your marketplace. As a product, do you stay in the same job or profession or seek out new growth options? With regard to your market, how do you need to consider your current industry or sector or are there other potential markets?

Thinking outside the box helps contextualise your efforts to framework your current reality.

Let's use the Product/Market Growth Matrix to think laterally about the possibilities or choices within each quadrant:

i. PERSONAL MARKET PENETRATION: CURRENT MARKET, CURRENT PRODUCT

Quadrant one has the lowest risk factor because you are familiar with both variables – your product (yourself and your competency portfolio) and your current market (your company and industry). To broaden your strategy means more ambition regarding promotion or progress in your current role and a more aggressive approach to penetrating your market with your current competencies. Whether you are an employee, self-employed, a business owner or an investor the more creativity you apply to penetrate your familiar marketplace the better.

More effective personal branding, salesmanship, marketing and widening your 'portfolio appeal' will contribute to increasing your potential from this quadrant. By simply brainstorming 20 ideas for improving how you can add more value or make more of an impact, you will come up with an improved growth plan. A career path development plan is an imperative in the corporate world. Getting a mentor to give you feedback and coaching is an imperative for the business owner.

In personal strategy formulation there are many ways to create the perception that you can add-value far in excess of what you are currently perceived as offering. Why not explore these other possibilities? Just one more way could dramatically improve your personal business offering. You may be just one skill or competency set away from the breakthrough you need to transform your situation.

ii. MARKET DEVELOPMENT: CURRENT PRODUCT, NEW MARKET

Market development – quadrant two – means that you will explore the options of a new market or industry within your current competency range, but at least one variable – your current competency portfolio – is familiar to you. To operate in this quadrant could involve bringing your current competency set to a fundamentally different place, like another country. Or another industry? Or a new market sector?

What is your strategy in this regard? Does it require investigation, research, and, above all, time to seek out a new opportunity? Are you watching the trends internationally? Surfing the net? Reading trade magazines? Attending conferences and trade shows? It's not urgent but it's always important to stay current in this age of information and communication.

Using every opportunity to dip your toe in the water as international projects come up may help you explore this growth option with the minimum of risk. One manager who moved 'lock, stock and barrel' to Australia to do the same job explained the lifestyle benefits as 'out of this world'. Another manager – a financial controller – changed her life by walking across the road to a new company and a new industry. The 'new culture' was everything she ever dreamed of.

iii. CAREER DIVERSIFICATION: NEW MARKET, NEW PRODUCT

Your third growth option – quadrant three – is high risk because you are developing new competencies in a new job or business and in a new market or industry. Putting a 'reinvented you' into a new market or industry you know nothing about can be like the 'blind leading the blind'. It is often a disastrous approach for small and medium business owners, but not always. The new energy may be the focus to propel you forward. Enter with care, caution and the necessary resources. An example is the corporate banker who left the financial treadmill in Dublin to open his own restaurant in the south of France. It was a great experience, if costly, but he returned home to more familiar territory after two years.

Keep in mind that 70 percent of the working population do not enjoy going to work primary because 'the fit' between *who they are* and *what they do* is a mismatch. Finding your vocation – doing work you love to do – is a life-long search for lots of people. Staying in a comfort zone is often easier than exploring options to find work closer to your heart's desire. The test is stress and the world of work is rife with stress which manifests itself in absenteeism, poor retention levels for companies and poor performance levels.

iv. Professional Development: New Product, Current Market

Professional development – quadrant four – is where you take the newly invented you (product) into your current market (company or industry). Obviously, the task of creating a whole new you, even with your established customers (boss), takes time and energy and the correct deployment of your current resources (e.g. time to do a degree, build critical competencies and learn the necessary knowledge). This is career change in a big way.

Significant professional development is often preceded by personal transformation. 'Project reinvent me' can be done by you on your own terms. Most people, however, get help through books, a course, a mentor, or a philosophy.

Entrepreneurs can reinvent themselves several times before hitting the big time after having two or three business failures. Perception, of course, can work for you or against you in this regard. Perception becomes the reality.

For example, one woman invested a small fortune in her own personal and professional development over several years only to find a glass ceiling – she called it an "iron door" – in her current job. She failed to convince the powers that be that she had changed and 'changed utterly'. They had her firmly 'boxed' or stereotyped. When she left the company she decided to confidently 'go for broke' and transformed her status and doubled her remuneration package in one fell swoop by selling her new energy factor. The lesson of course, is that the new you must be sold or you risk losing the opportunity at hand. Selling is a transfer of belief. Often 'your belief becomes my belief'. Perception is reality.

In summary, consider these ideas from the late great Peter Drucker, who said that "Marketing is the whole business seen from the point of view of its final result, that is, from the customer's point of view. Concern and responsibility for marketing must therefore permeate all areas of the enterprise". He added that "The purpose of marketing is to make selling unnecessary". How can you interpret these two powerful business statements and apply them to your personal and professional life? Who is your customer? What is the final result you seek? How are you marketing 'brand you'? Maybe you are trying too hard or overselling yourself?

1.10 SWOT ANALYSIS ... HOW DO YOU BUILD ON STRENGTHS AND MANAGE WEAKNESSES?

After your general overview, you can complete a personal and/or professional SWOT analysis to help pull all the elements together. SWOT is a good old fashioned strategy acronym for **S**trengths, **W**eaknesses, **O**pportunities and **T**hreats. Keep in mind that strengths and weaknesses are more internal and relative to 'similar others'. Opportunities and threats exist externally to your current activities. Most men and women know, almost instinctively, where their hot buttons and cold buttons are. The only problem is they have never written them up so these strengths and weaknesses can get the necessary attention. Furthermore, we seem to have a morbid fascination with 'what's wrong' with a person or situation rather than 'what's right' or where is the opportunity here? Learning to build on your strengths and manage your weaknesses is central to a strategy analysis. But first, you must clearly 'name' them so that all your focus goes into the right area.

In the personal strategy workbook, the SWOT analysis is diagnosed like this:

Strengths	Weaknesses
INTERNAL	
Opportunities	Threats
EXTERNAL	

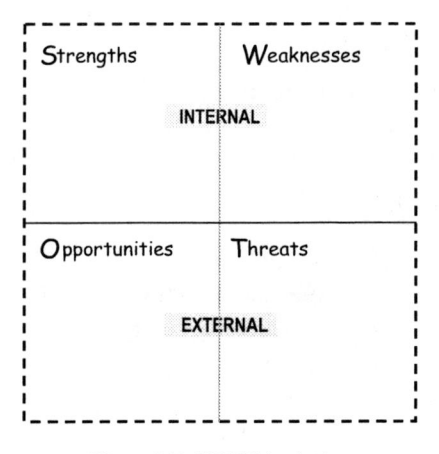

Figure 1.10 SWOT Analysis

A SWOT analysis can cover a multitude of parameters but your strengths and weaknesses are 80 percent internal and within your own control while opportunities and threats are 80 percent externally influenced. Add your own special areas. Here is a non-exclusive list of 11 areas to get you started:

i. **Talents And Competencies:** What are the talents – flair, gift, forte, genius – and personality factors that you can leverage off? Could you build on them if they are strengths? Are they holding you back because they are weaknesses? How do you define, measure and develop your levels of leadership, systems thinking, relationship building capability, action orientation, emotional intelligence?

   Technical competencies are often threshold competencies that get you into the job you hold but, thereafter, account for about 20 percent of the 'critical' success factors required to deliver superior performance in that job. It's the more personal leadership factors that are the block for most people. These are the most difficult to identify and, therefore, improve upon. If you don't know where your talents lie, how can you turn them into effective competencies?

ii. **Skills Inventory:** A skill is more narrowly defined than a talent. It suggests a degree of dexterity, aptitude, artistry, capability in a particular area. Have you distinguished the skill requirements for your job area or business? What about the hard skills such as computer literacy, financial acumen, production and marketing? What about the soft skills such as change management, coaching/mentoring, communication, delegation, negotiation, selling, report writing, problem solving, creativity and team building?

iii. **Processes, Functions, Roles:** Are your processes clear? At work, 80 percent of your problems – errors, reworks, delays, non-conformance to quality – will originate in your processes. Do you know your critical KRAs (Key Result Areas) and job definitions? Is your picture of your KRAs and your boss's picture the same? As a business owner what is your job? What can you delegate? To whom? What is your delegating process? Is your role clear to you and others? Do you need to change to a new role? Clarity and focus are your mantra words in this area.

iv. **Knowledge Management:** We live in the Information Age. Knowledge is the by-product of that age. Do you really know what you know? How informed are you with regard to marketing and sales, general business acumen, finance (cash flow), technology, strategic thinking and planning, networking and knowledge management? What are the essential 'chunks' of knowledge that you need to master to be highly regarded in your job? What would you need to know to be regarded as 'the obvious expert' in your field? What's stopping you from being the knowledge worker that turns raw information into valuable wisdom in your company? On the flipside, what information do you need to forget, get rid of and creatively abandon?

v. **Creativity and Innovation:** Your ability to introduce new ways of doing things is vital. Do you resist change? Innovation, change and marketing go hand-in-hand. How flexible are you relative to top performers in your industry? Even in other industries? Could your creativity and innovation be the seeds of an opportunity waiting to be taken? Do you ask for help? Would you be creative enough to ask the two most highly paid performers in your company or industry out to lunch for no other reason than to pick their brains? Creative intelligence is a way of thinking and acting that needs, above all, practice.

vi. **Physical Resources:** How modern and up-to-date is your personal equipment? Time remains one of your most valuable resources and it can be helped enormously by having a place at home where you can organise yourself. Electronic organisers are physical resources that need to be mastered to help build your strengths.

vii. **Personal Identity And Image:** Are you sending out the kind of messages that you want your '*audience*' to pick up? Are you consistent in delivering what you promise and how you promise it? How about your diary and paperwork? Is the appearance, colour and design of your office (inside and outside) consistent with the image you wish to convey? What about the quality, service, price and packaging of your product? What brand are you? What price are you? What are the words your '*customers*' would use to describe you? Is this how you want to be positioned? Products are made in factories, brands are created in people's minds. Are you a product or a brand? What is your image?

viii. **Quality Control:** What are the non-conformance levels in your area of management? What is the wastage? How much are your processes and systems contributing to poor internal communication? How much is poor communication '*really*' costing in terms of delays, lost customers and low morale? How much does all of this reflect on you? What have you done about it? Can you bring cost savings to quality control? Is delivery of quality work a strength, a weakness, an opportunity or a threat for you?

ix. **Production:** Can you improve throughput and quality? Can you reduce waste? Waste comes in many forms and shapes. Time is the most obvious. Raw material, energy and movement are others. Are you setting your benchmark against the best? Do you agree with this: '*Everyone is in sales*'. Are you in sales? What do you sell? What do you produce? Results? How could you produce your goods – whatever it is you produce – better, faster, cheaper, easier, newer, different? What competitive edge can you bring to bear on production? Is there an opportunity to double production in your area of influence in the next six months? How could you do it?

x. **Identification Of Critical Success Factors (CSFs):** What do you need to do really well to create strategic personal advantage? Do you know what your boss regards as your CSFs? Does each person in your team have their own CSFs? Do you know them? What are the biggest limiting factors in your team/business and what contribution are you making to bring solutions to solving them? Could your strengths be indicators of opportunities outside your current area of influence? Every job, every profession, every discipline on earth has 6-8 CSFs – all of which must be performed very well or enter the 'critical' state. If you were critically ill in hospital, for example, it means you could live or die. CSFs are live or die factors also. Bring 100 percent clarity to your CSFs.

xi. **Identification Of Choke Points:** A choke point is a constraint or limiting factor that prevents you from making best possible progress. What is your biggest weakness right now? Is it more tangible or intangible? If you eliminated this weakness, would it free up your whole system? Could you possibly be in denial about anything? What is the great unsaid? Who could tell you? Is it possible that you 'don't know' and as a result cannot name the offending choke point that is blocking you? How do you experience stress? Do you worry? What are you afraid to do? Have you ever asked for 360 degree feedback from those you know? What difference could it make? How important is *being right* to you? Could a choke point become a threat? Assume that 80 percent of your limiting factors are psychological in nature and that 20 percent are more technical in nature. Be careful not to allow the 20 percent to dominate the 80 percent.

In the corresponding workbook, spend time determining and isolating each SWOT area. An old proverb says "If you cannot name it you do not truly know it". Knowing your strengths, weaknesses, opportunities and threats is 'critical' to bringing clarity and focus to your strategy adventure.

1.11 EMERGING PRIORITIES FROM CURRENT SITUATION ANALYSIS

The more time you spend reflecting and reviewing your current place the better prepared you will be to map out your future strategy. You are always growing and changing. Becoming different. You are forever experimenting. In fact, everything is an experiment when you think about it. You are evolving even as you complete this exercise. Someone once said that "Action plus reflection is wisdom". Every hour you spend reflecting and collating your current position you will save 20 hours in strategy execution. So, if you spend the 100 recommended hours on the formulation part of this rubicon process you will save 2,000 hours when you come to the execution stage – that's like 12 months of the work year. This is the key to *crossing the rubicon* in personal strategy. Fundamental change over one year is irreversible and transformational.

Now that you have taken some action it is time to capture some of the 'big points' emerging for you as you read your own assessment of your current situation:
- What are you saying to yourself?
- What is the one big message emerging?
- What is the second big message?
- Is there a pattern emerging? What is it?

Write up six or 10 emerging priorities in your personal strategy workbook that you could craft into goals or action plans later in this process. This is a kind of summary action exercise to come back to later.

Lack of clarity and diffusion of effort are the two big saboteurs of progress in life and business. A thousand other issues get in the way if you are unclear and lack focus. The trivial things may keep you busy and knock out any hope of you getting time and attention to the vitally few important things.

Up to 80 percent of the blockages in your life are in your head and this is the single best way to sort out your thinking. This is why we have left no stone unturned in our effort to help you get a clear picture of your current situation.

Remember, sometimes you are only one skill or talent away from the breakthrough you deserve. Sometimes, a blinding flash of the obvious emerges from this current situation analysis. Sometimes one moment of insight can transform your thinking and circumstances for the better.

Now, for the next rubicon step ➡

RUBICON STEP 2

Reviewing Your History ... The Past

| RUBICON STEP 1 |
| CURRENT SITUATION ANALYSIS |

| **RUBICON STEP 2** |
| **REVIEWING YOUR HISTORY** |

| RUBICON STEP 3 |
| CLARIFYING & ORDERING VALUES |

| RUBICON STEP 4 |
| CRYSTALLISING YOUR MISSION |

| RUBICON STEP 5 |
| COMMITTING TO A CLEAR VISION |

| RUBICON STEP 6 |
| WRITING CLEAR STRATEGIC GOALS |

| RUBICON STEP 7 |
| TACTICAL PLANNING & IMPLEMENTATION |

"You are who you are ... you are also who you were: learn from the lessons of your history"

RUBICON STEP 2: REVIEWING YOUR HISTORY ... THE PAST

Your history review is an account of a whole series of past events connected with your life story. At this stage of your personal strategy formulation process, chronicle your story in narrative form as a report or tale or record of former times or the olden days. This should cover significant moments, key influences, successful strategic moves and the major contributing factors – positive and negative – that brought you to your current situation. Again, just start with a trigger phrase such as "*I was born ...*" or in your own preferred way.

Questions to consider: As your development path progressed what were the obstacles you encountered? And how have you grown and matured? Without understanding who you have been and what the journey so far has meant to you, it is difficult to focus on where you are going or should go. Your history is a key part of '*who you were*' and what you have become as well as '*what you do*' and who you prefer to do it with.

This exercise highlights the difference between the thinkers and planners of strategy. Strategic planners look at the past to find data points – milestones such as job changes – that allow them to uncover and plot trend lines. Your curriculum vitae, for example, is far too clinical to relay your life story. Strategic thinkers look back to uncover plot lines in order to decipher the moral of the story which helps to link your current reality with your soul – the inner you. Consider these questions: What have you learned from those bygone days? How did events impact on you then and now? How did you overcome setbacks and obstacles?

By understanding your past, you get a better sense of the present and the future. Your ability to rationalise the past empowers you to look three times as far forward into the future.

Consider the history step like a fishing expedition in five critical pools. These areas will give you vital information and the evidence you need to make more informed and sounder decisions for the future. Here are the five areas to write about:

FIVE AREAS TO EXPLORE

i. **Early Influences:** The first fishing pool leads you to consider some questions with regard to the early influences in your life. The central core of your character is built around your belief system which is formed in the family home and during your formative years. What are your memories – positive or negative – of your early upbringing and how do you feel this has influenced your development, maturity and personality? How influential were your parents in you becoming the person you are today? How much of your life to date and current personality is reflected in one or both of your parents? During your summer school holidays, what activities did you engage in? Overall, what influence has your early upbringing had on your life history?

ii. **School Years:** The second fishing pool worth exploring relates to your educational background and school experiences. You may have spent as long as 12-20 years in school and, obviously, it will have had a formidable impression on your character development and personality. Start off with primary school and move to secondary and third level as appropriate. What did you learn at school? How do you look back on your school life at this point? Did you complete all your courses and assignments? What would you do differently? What do you regret? What was school all about for you? What lasting impression did it leave on you? Did school leave you with a love for learning – so vital in the age of communication – or an apathy or distaste for learning?

iii. **Present Family Life:** The third fishing pool in which to 'cast your net' is your current life at home. You may have covered aspects of this in Current Situation Analysis (rubicon step 1). Where do you live? How did you come to live there? How do you live? Whom do you live with? How was this home unit formed? Do you live in a house or a home? What have been the joys and tribulations of living as you do? What has worked very well? What has not worked so well? Flesh it all out as best you can.

iv. **Health, Hobbies and Social Life:** How you spend your personal time can be a good indicator of who you really are. What are your accomplishments to-date in terms of sport, hobbies or other social activities? How is your health and what has been your medical history? Do you live a healthy lifestyle? How good have you been at achieving a work-life balance? The things you do in your spare time are a good indicator of *who you are* in that they are generally chosen freely and often can even be clues to your true talents. For example, a woman who describes herself as 'only a secretary' at work has demonstrated – as a volunteer – huge organisational and leadership competencies in an international sporting organisation over several years.

v. **Job and Career Assessment:** Work, job and career play a hugely influential role in most people's lives. So, start in chronological order with your first job, no matter how basic that first job was. Everyone starts somewhere and most people started helping out somewhere during the school holidays or working on a part-time basis. Go through each job, outlining the general roles and responsibilities that you carried out.

What were your hopes, aspirations and goals as you progressed through each job? What do you feel you achieved? How do you think each job served you in your development? How do you look back on the interaction with each company? What have you learned in terms of the critical jobs? What were your goals and objectives when you took the job in the first place? Why did you leave?

In your career to-date, what was your favourite job? Why? Which job did you like least? Why? What kind of circumstance, job or boss bring out the best in your performance? What really motivates you to best performance? Where have you been found wanting?

When you reflect on your career to-date, what irritates you? Consider a time when you were struggling in your career, how did you cope? Did you enjoy your work? Did you feel you were rewarded well enough? Knowing what you now know and with perfect 20/20 vision, what would you have done differently? What is the percentage of your performance-related-pay to your fixed salary? What have been your financial expectations and progress? Are you self-employed? Have you ever considered being your own boss? Why? Why not? Which asset class do you predominantly fall into – employee, self-employed, business owner or investor?

If you could wave a magic wand across your past jobs and careers, what one thing would you change? Where do you think you should be right now in terms of career progression or business achievement if you are self-employed? What is holding you back? What career-related or business things do you worry about on an ongoing basis?

These are character questions. They go to the very core of *who you are* and *what you do*. If you haven't made mistakes or have some regrets as you review this, then you haven't been trying hard enough. Mistakes mean you were bold and tried things. Expect to make more wrong turns in your future writing. Get over it and, more important, get on with it. Failures in your history merely demonstrate that you needed to learn some lessons.

STACKING UP THE EVIDENCE

Crossing the rubicon – your personal transformation journey – is like building evidence in a court case. Having collected all the evidence from your past, you can make better judgement calls regarding your current reality and future direction. In most cases, you are where you are today because of your past choices. Choices lead to consequences. And, of course, both success and failure leave tracks.

So, when you have completed this exercise in your personal strategy workbook, read it over and over and look for the patterns, rationalities and justifications you have made to defend your current position. Here are eight areas for you to consider:

i. **Emotional Maturity:** How you face the realities – especially the mishaps and mistakes – about your life and career path is probably the best indicator of your level of emotional maturity. Consider these patterns and choices: When things go wrong, who do you tend to blame or do you generally face obstacles and challenges in a positive way? Have you got big hang-ups and regrets about the past or do you just skip over it and keep looking to the future?

When someone 'displays a maturity beyond their years' it means they show a high degree of level-headedness, wisdom, shrewdness and discrimination. Emotional maturity is about taking responsibility for all the episodes of your life. How much time do you spend looking over your shoulder at the past compared to how goal-oriented you are about the future? How well do you accept criticism and feedback or is this an area you are defensive about? Who or what 'pushes your buttons'? Are you a taker or a giver? Ultimately the giver gains.

What are the indicators of immaturity? Immature people blame other people when things go wrong and make excuses for their own inability to do what needs to be done. They say things like *"if only ... then I would ..."* or *"I have always been this way ..."*. Immature people tend to get depressed and irrational when criticised. They attack and defend irrationally, sometimes on irrelevant issues. They may take 'macho' strong positions on how things are and how things may be done. Immaturity puts a break on future progress. Learning to take full responsibility is the antidote to emotional immaturity.

ii. **Achievement Orientation:** How achievement oriented are you, really? Look for the evidence in your level of goal setting, persistence and tenacity throughout your past life. Look for patterns of success in your ability to get results and overcome obstacles to reach goals and your ability to complete tasks. Do you have a history of not completing things? Are you actively working towards achieving your goals and objectives in your present job? Did you finish off all your courses and degrees?

Consider some very difficult assignments you have undertaken. Did you complete them? Be careful of selective responsibility here. In other words, beware of extremism, which can be an indication of immaturity. Are your traits of persistence and tenacity tempered with realism and maturity?

iii. **Authority Conflict:** As you look back through your written history and current situation analysis, watch out for motivators that suggest you have a tendency to resist or fight authority. This may manifest itself in a tendency to criticise or belittle successful people and is often identified in how you view your parents. Did you seem to have ongoing clashes or disagreements with parents, teachers, supervisors or bosses?

Is everyone out of step except you? For example, if you have had a difficulty with your father or a teacher, you may mirror that authority conflict with your boss. It's called projection. By becoming aware of this and establishing the level of this conflict, you can un-hook from it and control these patterns for the future. Otherwise you are destined to repeat the mistakes of the past. People join a company and leave a boss. However, in most cases, your boss has been sent to you as a gift to help you deal with the conflict within yourself that has been left unresolved.

iv. **Mental Stability:** Your degree of mental stability is best demonstrated by your 'balance of mind', degree of normality and sense of reason. You will find evidence of stability from strong relationships with people, places, jobs, occupations, hobbies and from your life's journey and track record. Evidence of instability can stem from a troubled childhood, a dysfunctional home, a less than pleasant school life or a marriage break-up. Being self-aware and alert to this emerging evidence can be very important to your future progress. Ironically, someone who has spent a number of years with one company could indicate lack of growth and even indicate stagnation.

v. **Self-Image:** Your self-image is like a current snapshot or balance sheet of *who you are* and *what you do*. It's your reputation with yourself. It's how you appreciate and how much you like yourself. There is a psychological principle that suggests there is a corresponding relationship between your current reality on the outside and how you think and feel on the inside. As within, so without. Can you reel back the years and undo destructive experiences? In your mind, you can change your self-concept and kill off the demons of the past.

vi. **Hardiness Test:** How robust and sturdy would you say you are really? How would you rate your resilience and fortitude in living through the critical events of your life and stressful situations? Look at your most traumatic life experience: How did you cope? How would you rate your level of street wisdom and hardiness? Take your worst failure: What happened? What was the outcome? What did you do? How do you view failure? How much ruggedness and stamina do you feel you have?

vii. **Locus Of Control:** The psychological principle of control says that you are happy or unhappy to the degree that you are in control of the sequence of events and circumstances as they unfold in your life. Do you understand the difference between eu-stress (positive stress) and out of control stress? How much stress have you taken on board as you read your history? How much worry? Was it necessary? What have you learned?

Psychosomatic symptoms of stress may include headache, insomnia, backache, ulcers, high blood pressure, nervous breakdown and irritability. Is there any evidence that you are living in fear of what might happen around the next corner? In other words, is your locus of control internal or external? Where is mission control for you?

viii. **Personal Values:** A personal value is something that is important and significant to you as a human being. Personal values are based on beliefs, principles, ethics, moral values, standards and codes of behaviour. Honesty and integrity are always at the core of a personal values system. So consider how honest a person you are. Do you keep your promises and commitments? Do you face reality?

IN REVIEWING YOUR HISTORY

Shakespeare defines integrity as 'to thine own self be true'. Integrity has been described as the value that guarantees all other values. How does it sit with your review of your history?

Having reviewed your own history and current situation, can you detect any contradictions, doubts, double statements, patterns that don't quite add up? What happened to you is a fact of life. How you choose to look back on it is, however, within your own control.

Consider now, how you have analysed your childhood and school years. Have you written your history through the lens of success, growth and progress? Are there role models there? Are there heroes? How did you explain, express and emotionalise your successes and failures during your development?

Is there any evidence that you have been engaging in self-sabotage by opting out of key tasks and assignments? Who are you still blaming for your current reality? Nearly getting there? Incomplete assignments? Denial? Lots of verbal spoof and excuses as to why it never really worked out for you? What stopped you?

Is it time to reconcile the past with the present reality and future possibilities? 'Listen' to your written words carefully. You have left all the evidence with all the tracks necessary to transform the next part of your journey, if that needs to happen. Edward R. Murrow once said that "Difficulty is the excuse history never accepts".

The current situation and historical analysis involved in the rubicon process is a form of self-revelation, self-awareness and self-development, all rolled into one. When you truly engage with the first two steps of the rubicon process, you somehow seem capable of looking twice as far into the future as those who do not.

Now, for the next rubicon step ➡

RUBICON STEP 3

Clarifying & Ordering Your Values ... The Why

RUBICON STEP 1
CURRENT SITUATION ANALYSIS

RUBICON STEP 2
REVIEWING YOUR HISTORY

RUBICON STEP 3
CLARIFYING & ORDERING VALUES

RUBICON STEP 4
CRYSTALLISING YOUR MISSION

RUBICON STEP 5
COMMITTING TO A CLEAR VISION

RUBICON STEP 6
WRITING CLEAR STRATEGIC GOALS

RUBICON STEP 7
TACTICAL PLANNING & IMPLEMENTATION

"Values shape your character, energise your talents and fast-forward your decision-making capability"

RUBICON STEP 3: CLARIFYING & ORDERING VALUES ... THE WHY

Values are at the very heart of what makes you competent and strategically focused. Values energise your talents and help align them with your purpose and destiny. Values shape your character. Your values are the fuel in the fire of your personal strategy. Your core values determine *who you are* and how you do *what you do*. Your values are at the very epicentre of your 'being'.

A personal value can be described as 'what is important and significant to you as a human being'. Values are your core belief system and crystallise your perception of 'what is right' for you.

Personal values are procedures – more like habits – that do not depend on fear to put into practice. Personal freedom and choice are the essential bedrock of values. You can, of course, learn to implement a new value simply by practicing it in every possible situation. Charles Reade wrote "Sow an act, and you reap a habit. Sow a habit and you reap a character. Sow a character and you reap a destiny".

What role do values play in strategy formulation and *crossing the rubicon*? Values provide a framework for decision-making in your life. They also provide a basis for action and help you to live with the results of your actions. Values are your unifying principles and core beliefs and provide the anchor point of personal strategy. Thomas Jefferson said "In matters of principle, stand like a rock". When you bring clarity to *who you are* on the *inside*, only then can you determine a clear focus on the *outside* to your future direction.

All improvements in your personal or professional development begin by clarifying and ordering your true values and then committing yourself to live by them. James Allen once said "All that there is to making a successful, happy and beautiful life is the knowledge and application of simple root principles".

Everyone has a value system whether it's good or bad, clear or unclear. Most people have never explored their core values in a meaningful way. On the other hand, value-driven men and women achieve clarity, have vision and set long-term strategic goals to realise their vision. As Joan Baez put it "You don't get to choose how you are going to die. Or when. You can decide how you're going to live. Now".

In the world of business the core values of an organisation can determine its culture and way of doing business. Too often, however, rules, laws and procedures set boundary lines such as: 'If you break this rule you will be penalised' or 'You will be in trouble if …'. Negative cultures breed fear and inhibitions and takes endless time to police. Positive cultures empower people to be more creative and productive.

"All that is necessary for the triumph of evil is that good men do nothing" are the immortal words of Edmund Burke in the 18th century. Civilisations, like the Roman Empire and modern societies like the American and French Republics' are anchored on core value systems encapsulated in the powerful words of their constitutions. Most democratic principles are timeless, universal, even eternal value statements.

Australia is rethinking its attitude to values. "Before becoming an Australian, you will be asked to subscribe to certain values. If you do not like those values, don't come to Australia" are the words of Peter Costello, a senior minister in the Australian government.

Europe, too, is being challenged by the values it holds. In a 2006 Pew survey, 50 percent of Italians considered Islam to be "a religion more fanatical than any other". In Switzerland, 25 percent of the population considered Muslims a threat to their country. The Pew poll found that 51 percent of the Dutch viewed Muslims unfavourably. The caricaturing of Mohammed in early 2006 by Danish Cartoonists triggered widespread rioting and caused over 100 deaths. "The notion of multi-culturalism has fallen apart" says Angela Merkel, the German chancellor. "Anyone coming here must respect our constitution and tolerate our western and Christian roots". Values appreciation lies at the very core of these challenges. Core freedoms emerge when crises present themselves.

Hippocrates – the father of medicine – set the first medical values over 2,000 years ago when he advised doctors to "Primum non nocere" (First, do no harm). Mahatma Gandhi (1869-1948) crystallises the importance of values as follows: "It's the action, not the fruit of the action that's important. You have to do the right thing. It may not be in your power, it may not be in your time, that there'll be any fruit. But that does not mean you stop doing the right thing. You may never know what results from your action. But if you do nothing, there will be no result".

Focus is the key ingredient of all good strategy. Champions in sport practice focus. Practitioners of martial arts become experts on focus. The secret of karate is that all the energy and force is centred on a very small area such as the edge of your hand. That's why black-belt karate experts can smash through stacks of boards or bricks without pain. All psychological and physical energy is totally focused on the breakpoint.

If someone threw a basin of water over you, you would get very wet. But if the same water were shot at you through a high-powered water hose gun, you might also get injured. The only difference is concentrated power and focus.

The real foundation of a happy, healthy, self-confident lifestyle is living a life consistent with your core values. When you have total clarity and inner acceptance in this area, you accept yourself unconditionally as a valuable and worthwhile person and this is what fuels your strategy.

So, what are your personal and professional values? All the great values are simple and can often be expressed in a single word or short phrase. What is your attitude to risk? To achieving high performance? What about growth, resource deployment, independence, equality, contribution, duty, family, community, honour, people, teamwork, hope, profit, freedom of action, freedom of speech, communication, mercy, quality, health and safety, remuneration, innovation, justice, learning, ethical standards, the environment, public service, responsibility, clarity?

How Do You Write A Set Of Values?

The mechanics of engaging in a values exercise is relatively simple. In the personal strategy workbook, just brainstorm key words and phrases that constitute your personal and professional values. Good questions to help trigger your thoughts are:

- What do you do that gives you the most pride?
- What is really satisfying about *what you do*?
- What do you stand for/What do you not stand for?
- What do you hold dear?
- What do you really value?

The next part of the exercise is to craft the key words and phrases into Value Statements. Just follow the forced response methodology in the workbook to help you. This can be more difficult, but it's where emotional strategy really comes alive.

Here is an example of a set of personal values.

My core values are:

1. To live my life with honesty and integrity
2. To be excellent in all my family relationships
3. To be financially independent
4. To enjoy my career to its fullest.

A personal value statement is often a simple, straight-forward encapsulation of the obvious. The order is important, however.

You need to consider alternatives/options and grade them in order of importance. Ranking them in order of importance is an imperative. Why? If you do not, you can trade one off against the other. In the example above, nothing supercedes 'honesty and integrity'. In this example, integrity is first and foremost, then family, then money, then career. If this person were to throw away three, the one kept would be integrity. This is the test. Do you feel good about these values? Are you happy to talk publicly about your value positions and views?

You will find that all the successful applications of the elements of this rubicon strategy emerge from a clear understanding of your values.

It's important that you choose your values without influence from anyone else. It's important that they need to be consistent and in harmony with one another.

Here is another example of a values statement:

1. To respect myself as a valuable and worthwhile human being
2. To actively work at my roles as a 'good' wife, mother, daughter and citizen
3. To reach my full potential in my work life
4. To 'give back' to those who are less fortunate.

The 'obvious things' that are not before your eyes are easy to forget, especially in times of crises. Great nations have values, embedded in their charters or constitutions. Great companies have values that empower people with the freedom and guidelines to contribute better. Individuals that want to *cross the rubicon* need to identify, rank and live by their values.

A miscellaneous, unordered list of values that may help you to begin this process is given below.

honesty	involvement in politics
integrity	religious beliefs
professional success	good manners
open-mindedness	individual freedom
success and achievement	winning
family happiness and success	law and order
keeping my thinking on social issues	orderly home life
standing firm on matters of principle	being decisive
friendship	having a balanced life style
financial independence	musical excellence
peace of mind	self-sufficiency
marital harmony	credibility in my profession
being creative	doing something worthwhile
health and energy	serving the less well-off
keeping careful records	loving relationships
being a leader	understanding other people
intellectual growth	being a good listener
personal excellence	trust in God
freedom of speech	tolerance of others
being a good team player	artistic talent
ability to make things happen	dressing well
my problem-solving ability	my influencing ability
being purposeful	discipline
my sense of fairness	being a risk-taker
preparing my children for adulthood	being patriotic
street-wisdom	common-sense

Many people struggle with conflicting values. The act of committing your values to paper and reviewing them on a regular basis separates the competent from the incompetent. Written-down values provide parameters for deciding on a position more quickly. They help you to leapfrog procrastination, fear of failure and negativity blocks. They help with communication, motivation, strategy and learning. You feel happy and content. This allows you to focus on higher order work and worthwhile achievements. Clarifying and ordering your values is, ultimately, a statement of how you will live your life from this moment in time.

Now, for the next rubicon step ➝

RUBICON STEP 4

Crystallising Your Mission ... The What

RUBICON STEP 1
CURRENT SITUATION ANALYSIS

RUBICON STEP 2
REVIEWING YOUR HISTORY

RUBICON STEP 3
CLARIFYING & ORDERING VALUES

**RUBICON STEP 4
CRYSTALLISING YOUR MISSION**

RUBICON STEP 5
COMMITTING TO A CLEAR VISION

RUBICON STEP 6
WRITING CLEAR STRATEGIC GOALS

RUBICON STEP 7
TACTICAL PLANNING & IMPLEMENTATION

"What is your life all about? What is your purpose? What is your calling? How are you going about doing what you have to do?"

RUBICON STEP 4: CRYSTALLISING YOUR MISSION ... THE WHAT

Your mission statement should be a broadly-based enduring statement of purpose that distinguishes you from 'similar others'. It explains the reason for your long-term existence. It crystallises and articulates your values, dreams and behaviours. It is about how you aspire to do things. It's your operational, ethical and fundamental guiding light.

Your mission statement should define your purpose in life. Your mission becomes a way of life for you, almost like a vocation. It should explain *who you are* with *what you do*, where you are coming from with *where you are going*. When you are 'working on purpose' you are happy and 'in the zone'. People with purpose rarely 'go to work'. Work instead becomes full of meaning and direction. In a nutshell, it's what you are about.

Crafting your mission statement is a relatively simple task if you follow a system. Capturing your thoughts in the form of words is the big challenge. It's like writing your legacy in advance. Your mission, of course, should evolve from your values statement. Herbert Casson, the philosopher, once wrote "To have a purpose that is worthwhile and that is steadily being accomplished, that is one of the secrets of a life that is worth living".

Your mission statement encapsulates the answers to the questions: *'What is your calling?' 'What is life all about?' 'Who are you?' 'How are you going about doing what you have to do?'* It captures the driving forces of your internal engine in one simple sentence.

Crafting the mission statement from a mixed bag of descriptive words and phrases and distilling these words into one cogent sentence is often a soul-searching, but rewarding exercise. This exercise is at the core of strategic thinking and planning on a personal or professional level.

There has been much confusion and many conflicting opinions about the difference between a mission and a vision. However, when following the rubicon model, it's important that you are clear about these definitions:

Mission is your long-term purpose.

Vision (rubicon step 5) is what you can 'visualise and see' at a particular time in the future. It's your biggest goal. More on vision later.

RUBICON STEP 4: Crystallising Your Mission ... The What

Corporate groups can spend hours arguing over words and phrases that best represent what they are about. They soon realise that many of their troubles and weaknesses are caused by the different and diverse assumptions and beliefs of each individual and group.

Here are some examples of personal mission statements:

- "My purpose in life is to listen to and develop my own special calling in social care and to help other people live happier lives with this gift"

- "My ultimate mission in the world is to make a significant difference in the lives of the less fortunate"

- "My mission is to live a life full of integrity and challenge, starting with myself and my family, then my work colleagues and the wider community"

- "My mission is to achieve my full potential as a professional and be fully alive in doing this"

Writing a mission brings clarity, focus and power to your current reality and future direction. Lack of clarity and diffused effort are the primary causes of poor performance, lost opportunity and stress.

When you write down your enduring statement of purpose, you are forced to meet yourself on the page. After several, sometimes many, drafts and edits, your sixth sense knows that this form of words sums you up.

Over time, your mission helps you develop a quiet confidence and a steel-like strength to handle the challenges that life throws at you. Type it up, put it in your wallet with a photo of your loved ones and read it at odd moments in time to confirm you are living on purpose.

Animals are supplied at birth with the instincts to survive and thrive. That's why creatures in the animal kingdom don't need the same brainpower as humans. In the *Secret of Freedom*, the playwright Archibald MacLeish says "The only thing different about a man that is man is his mind. Everything else you can find in a pig or a horse". Think about how true that is! Ultimately, you are a mind with a physical body to carry you around.

Unfortunately, most people do not know how to use their mind and therefore do not appreciate the power that clarity of purpose plays in achieving their personal potential. If mankind had depended on instinct and muscle for survival,

CROSSING THE RUBICON: Seven Steps To Writing Your Own Personal Strategy

you probably would now be an extinct creature, just like the dinosaurs which were the most physically powerful creatures that ever lived. So, tap into your brain-power. Leave the brawn-power and survive-on-instinct to the animals.

Beware of the cynic within you that scoffs at such an exercise. Be aware that the laughter of others is their defence mechanism as to their rationale for not completing such an exercise. In other words, be clear as to the importance of writing a mission. Then take courage and just do it.

One of the big regrets for many older people is that they do not bring clarity and focus to their mission in life much earlier as crystallised in the immortal words of Oliver Wendell Holmes "Most people die with their music still in them".

Now, for the next rubicon step ➡

RUBICON STEP 5

Committing To A Clear Vision
... The Future

| RUBICON STEP 1 |
| CURRENT SITUATION ANALYSIS |

| RUBICON STEP 2 |
| REVIEWING YOUR HISTORY |

| RUBICON STEP 3 |
| CLARIFYING & ORDERING VALUES |

| RUBICON STEP 4 |
| CRYSTALLISING YOUR MISSION |

| **RUBICON STEP 5** |
| **COMMITTING TO A CLEAR VISION** |

| RUBICON STEP 6 |
| WRITING CLEAR STRATEGIC GOALS |

| RUBICON STEP 7 |
| TACTICAL PLANNING & IMPLEMENTATION |

"What does your future hold for you? The impossible dream? The unknown? The perfect opportunity?"

RUBICON STEP 5: COMMITTING TO A CLEAR VISION ... THE FUTURE

A vision is a clear description of a desired state of affairs at a particular moment in the future. Your vision is your big goal, your magnificent obsession, your major definite purpose for the next three-to-five years, maybe longer. It brings clarity and focus to your values and mission statements. Your vision statement should:

• Focus on the operational side of your life

• Have clear measurable objectives and be results orientated

• Change your primary focus over the next 3-5-10 years.

Elbert Hubbard once wrote that "The great secret of success is that there is no secret of success". But your courage to envision your future is the characteristic that ranks most highly when leadership attributes are discussed. All the great leaders of the past are characterised by the vision they had. Now it's your turn to write your vision for the future.

As a yardstick, your vision statement should give you an easy answer to the questions 'Where, exactly, am I going?' and 'Am I there yet?' Being crystal clear about your future direction and fuelled by a passion to get you there are massive motivators for a human being. Animals don't think about, plan for or dream about the future. In simple terms, your ability to think and visualise is what separates humans from all other creatures.

Your vision statement is a rallying cry 'It will be great when I get there, so ...'. There is nothing like a vision to release your energies, if it is clear, specific, time-bounded and realistic. It is only for your own eyes or those very near to you.

Everything, however, is dependent on the execution of your vision. A vision without execution is just a dream. It says in the *Bible* that "Without a vision the people will perish". Without a vision you will lack motivation and be prisoner to self-doubt and stress. Without a vision your purpose and values cannot be activated.

A good example of a vision that was fulfilled was President John F. Kennedy's vision in 1961 of "Achieving the goal, before this decade is out, of landing a man on the moon and returning him safely to Earth". This statement had the five essentials of a great vision. It was **S**pecific, **M**easurable, **A**chievable, **R**esults-oriented and **T**ime-bounded (SMART). Your vision statement today should have a three-to-five year time frame with an eye on 10-20 years also.

Before taking a decision on any significant personal or professional issue you should, after you write your vision, ask yourself two questions:

1. Is this decision consistent with my values, mission and vision?

2. Is this action/decision I am about to make big enough or strong enough to help me towards the realisation of my vision?

Your vision helps integrate and synchronise *who you are* with *what you do* and *where you are going*. It allows you to dream big dreams. To be bold. Imagineering is the art and science of tapping into the core of your psyche, your subconscious mind. Trust yourself. Just do it. Visioning is art and learned science. Practice helps. What is the most constant recurring picture in your mind? What do you dream about at night and day-dream about during the day? What does your 'chatter-box' keep asking of you? These are clues to your vision.

When finalising your vision, consider the words of Pope John Paul II: "Consult not your fears but your hopes and dreams. Think not about your frustrations, but about your unfulfilled potential. Concern yourself not with what you tried and failed in, but what it is still possible for you to do."

Imagination or dreaming is the ability to form a mental image of something that is not perceived through the normal senses. It is the ability of the mind to build mental scenes, objects or events that do not exist, are not present or have happened in the past. Dreams are inspirational. They ignore obstacles and envisage positive outcomes. "I have just realised my childhood dream" is how one Olympic champion captured the realisation of his ambition after winning a gold medal.

So what is a dream? 'To dream something up' means to invent, concoct, devise, hatch or create something. 'Your dream home' is your ideal, perfect, even fantasy home. Colloquialisms such as "I wouldn't dream of being late" or "She is a right day-dreamer" or "He's a dream to work with" help us capture the meaning of the term dream. It conjures up images of hope, intention, desire, wish, yearning, wonder, gem, and, of course, vision. Dreams are therefore a series of thoughts, images and sensations from deep inside your subconscious mind that occur while you sleep or while you daydream. The immortal words "I have a dream" of Martin Luther King on 28th August 1963, at a Civil Rights march sums up 'the dream thing' for everybody: "I have a dream that one day on the red hills of Georgia, the sons of former slaves and the sons of former slave owners will be able to sit down together at the table of brotherhood".

All successful men and women have a dream which can be turned into a clear vision. A vision includes a vivid image of what you want to achieve in your life or career and incorporates meaningful extensions of the values you feel passionate about. A dream is a hope and hope is never a strategy. A vision is more concrete. You can 'sell' a vision. It's a more mental image as opposed to a more emotional state of a dream. Passion is the vital energy that can help turn a vision into reality. Your vision and what you feel passionate about need to be strongly connected and it should incorporate your biggest financial or personal goals and allow you to show-case your talents.

Having a clear vision makes it easier to take focused action. If you do not, you essentially allow outside factors to determine your success. You effectively work to someone else's agenda. The vision acts as a kind of sieve that filters out all the distractions that often seem important but, actually, don't serve the bigger picture.

Creating a vision is about taking firm control of your future and accepting responsibility for the definite choices you need to make. A good vision is the best way to make all your dreams come true.

THE BEHAVIOURS OF THE GREAT VISIONARIES

Great visionaries behave in certain consistent ways. These behaviours are often obvious, simple and learnable, but *knowing* about them and *doing* something about them is the difference between the amateur and the professional, the winner and the also ran.

On the negative side, call it your fatal flaw, blind spot or limiting factor that stops you from reaching your potential. On the positive side, it's the search for the winning edge, being brilliant on the basics or the tipping point. Consider these 10 questions regarding your vision:

i. **How Do You Entertain Your Dreams?** The line from the Joe Darion song in the 1960s "The Impossible Dream" challenges you to dream the big dream. Another singer, Glen Campbell, sang "I've got dreams to dream and songs to sing in the morning ... I've got everything a man could ever need". All visions of the future start with a dream. All great buildings and achievements happened in someone's mind first. In other words, you have to have a dream if you want to make a dream come true. What about your dream job? What would it look like? Visualise yourself in it. Imagine what your life would be like if you doubled, quadrupled or increased your income by six times. What steps could you take right now to move towards that vision?

ii. **Are You Building On Your Talents?** When you are working in harmony with your natural talents, you get all the motivation you need to achieve your vision and goals. Get good at what you love to do, then get better, then differentiate yourself by being exceptional in that field. Build on your strengths, invest in your talent. Ironically, when you are fulfilling your 'hearts desire' the concept of work no longer exists. Work becomes an old fashioned idea. A job becomes a term that you do not understand. The majority of people never set a vision because they don't enjoy what they do enough to get really good at it and so never reap the rewards that visionaries achieve. Mediocrity is their calling card. They constantly battle with the job/work idea. The search for excellence is your calling card.

iii. **Do You Take 100 percent Responsibility For Your Life?** All visionaries take ownership of their vision. They look and feel like the boss. They have a self-employed attitude regardless of who pays them. Taking responsibility means no more excuses and no blaming other people for your situation. You are where you are today because of your own actions or inactions. You are responsible. You must take control of your own vision. Turn it into a 'magnificent obsession' if you must. Otherwise, your destiny is to help someone else achieve their vision. Consider how you could perform if you owned all the equity in your company! Consider how committed you would be if your life depended on it. Responsibility spells two words, *respond* and *ability*, or your *ability* to *respond*.

iv. **Why Haven't You Achieved This Vision Already?** What is stopping you? Are you risk-averse? Consider the worst possible outcome of seriously embarking on the road to achieving your vision. Then, put the plans in place to ensure 'the worst' does not happen. Fear is the biggest single 'block' to getting started. Fear provides the good excuse that protects you from failure. Failure is sent to instruct not obstruct. Failure is necessary for success. Failure, of course, is only an opportunity to begin again – more intelligently – because there is no security in life, only opportunity. Look at the vision you would like to achieve and ask yourself "Has anyone else already achieved such an objective? Who? When"? The *already* question frees you up to start taking the steps to achieve the vision.

v. **Are You Prepared To Work Hard Over Time?** Working eight hours a day is for putting bread on the table. All visionaries take a long-term perspective and, therefore, have no difficulty investing 50-70 hours per week over many years to achieve their goals. The media image of the swashbuckling 25 year old billionaire is a long way from the reality. It's a Hollywood image and can frighten more than motivate. The average millionaire takes 22 years to become financially independent and is 48 years old before they become wealthy. Hard work, however, is like play because of the high level of motivation and enjoyment they get from the pursuit of 'the vision thing'. The get rich quick mentality is anathema to the true visionary.

vi. **What Words Sum Up Your Personal Brand?** Your reputation for action, dependability, speed, execution, professionalism, integrity, reliability, efficiency can be some of the brand terms that differentiate you from the rest of the pack. What is your brand mark? How would your best customer refer to you in a conversation? How would you want them to talk about you? What do you need to do to create an image of uniqueness about yourself? What kind of 'promise' do you exude? How do you live up to or down to that promise? The chairman of a board was asking why the key members of

RUBICON STEP 5 : Committing to a Clear Vision ... The Future

the board had appointed the new CEO. He replied "His reputation for making things happen ... results orientation". Every action adds to, or takes away from, your personal brand. Make sure your actions are consistent and that you implicitly or explicitly keep the promises you make. Getting a reputation for being reliable and trustworthy, for example, is a great platform for positioning yourself as an expert.

vii. **How Much Discipline Have You?** Napoleon Hill studied the wealthiest men and women for more than 20 years and concluded that "Self-discipline is the master key to riches". Vision-discipline is the practice of following the rules and behaviours that have proved to be successful for visionary-achievers. Thomas Huxley defined discipline as "Doing what you should do, when you should do it, whether you like it or not". Consider all your tendencies to waste time and procrastinate in the 168 hours you have each week. You only work 40-60 of those hours with another 50-60 hours for sleep, so what do you do with the other 60-70 hours that could advance your vision? You can get good at anything from beekeeping to micro-biology in about 50 hours ... that's one hour per week over a year. You could become an expert on a subject with about 1,000 hours. And you could become an authority in about 5,000 hours. Discipline and time go hand in hand.

viii. **How Decisive Are You?** Consider this: Only one third of your decisions will be completely right, one third will be wrong and not capable of being rescued or made right, and one third will be wrong with the possibility of making other decisions to save them. How decisive are you? How flexible are you? How quick can you admit to your mistakes and move on? Do you understand that any decision is better than no decision in most cases? Where are you stuck? Why? What do you need to do about it? Decisiveness is an essential attribute of all good strategists. Being decisive comes in many forms depending on the need and circumstances.

ix. **How Good Are You At Service?** You are in sales in the sense that you influence, persuade and communicate with a myriad of people all the time.

CROSSING THE RUBICON: Seven Steps To Writing Your Own Personal Strategy

How good are you at follow-up, follow-through, adding-value? How good are you at going the extra mile? How often do you do more than you are paid for? How good are you on the details? Visionaries are constantly selling and giving service to others. In fact, helping other people achieve their goals and dreams is one of the best ways you can achieve your vision. Very few people can do it on their own. Who do you serve? Who do you need to serve better? Who do you need to get to know? Moments of service, of course, come in many forms, from basic delivery which has minimal impact to exceptional delivery which leaves a lasting impression.

x. **Are You A Learner?** Someone once said that you can "Ask your way to the top" by being an alert listener, and having the wisdom to seek out the information you need to get any task completed. Visionaries are askers. Visionaries are learners. Visionaries read, listen, observe, question and tell stories. Visionaries tell stories to paint pictures of desired future outcomes more to reinforce the picture in their own head than to impress someone they are talking to. How good are you at painting pictures, selling concepts or telling stories? Visionaries encounter obstacles all the time but view them as mere learning episodes. Inherently, they embrace their own experiences as just part of the journey.

VISION STATEMENTS

Here is a case study of a company vision statement: A business owner with a turnover of €15m wrote a vision statement several years ago for his company 'To be the best in our industry.' His colleagues thought it was a great statement. In reality it was meaningless, and at most, a mere slogan. It could not be realised. Every competitor today tells their customers 'We are the best' in some way or other. Even those who are not the best often redefine the industry boundaries to ensure they can make this claim. It was not time-bounded. It was not specific. It had no meaning or fire power. No wonder it didn't focus or energise them.

By the time the company had completed their strategy process their vision was:

'To grow our company to €150m turnover, with a net profit of five percent by opening four new branches, developing our staff to 75 people by 30th December 2012'

Everyone was excited about this. Apprehensive? Yes. Sceptical? Sure. All kinds of potential opportunity beckoned. Focused team work prevailed.

Here are three examples of personal vision statements:

• "My vision is to achieve a net worth of €2 million primarily by building a property portfolio and creating a passive rental income (outside my job) of €75,000 per year by 3rd December 2010"

• "My personal vision is to buy and live on a farm of 100 acres in my home county of Wexford by April 10th 2009"

• "My vision is to live out some of my dreams over the next five years as follows:

1. To play golf on 10 of the top PGA recognised golf courses in the world. (Two big courses each year).

2. To sell my business for a minimum of €30 million, preferably through an MBO by 17th March 2010.

3. To redirect my work focus to 10% community work, 30% free time, 30% investor and 30% attention to my business by the end of 2011.

These examples of personal vision statements may serve to give you some ideas and, more importantly, some parameters for your own statement. Someone once said that "When you see clearly what is there, you have set the platform to create insights into what is not there". This is why the whole process up to now was a mere prelude to the main event – the vision. Write your vision statement.

CRITICAL SUCCESS FACTORS OF THE VISION STATEMENT

Vision critical success factors (CSFs) are written 'memos to yourself' that encapsulate the driving forces between your vision and your strategic goals (rubicon step 6). They are strategic intent statements that bring clarity and focus to some general objective areas. They should help change the odds in your favour, relative to your colleagues or competitors.

A VISION CSF is an expression of strategic intent, a desired leadership position and a declared policy to yourself. It creates a sense of 'this is what I have to do to win the strategy game' whilst leaving a high degree of flexibility for execution purposes.

The consistent strategy that will make your Vision possible and achievable is made-up of these VISION CSFs. Some examples are:

- **Leadership Development:** My intention is to become an exceptional leader. I realise this is a journey but the phrase that most inspires me is "that leaders are learners". In other words, leaders are *made* more than born. Over the next five to 10 years, I intend to invest the time and money in my own leadership development by reading extensively (books, book summaries, magazines), listening to audio/CD material (e-learning CDs, videos, DVDs), joining selected institutes and organisations for networking purposes (IoD, IBA), and actively seeking coaching and mentoring from certain role models (MB, JC).

- **Computer Literacy:** My intention is to master – once and for all – the basics, and then the more advanced operations of my PC. I will need to get help in this area by attending classes or reading the manuals. This is my limiting factor right now. I must make it my strongest asset. I really need to get a coach to dedicate fixed hours to concentrate on mastering this neglected area for me.

Other VISION CSF category focus areas may be: Financial literacy, continuous professional development, personal development, technical qualifications, travel, hobbies, home/house, networking, image, community, business, health, wealth, success, family, relationships, public speaking, politics, sport. The category possibilities are as wide as you need.

Written correctly, VISION CSFs are like 'memos or instructions to yourself' suggesting or challenging you to incorporate these objectives into your more specific strategic goals over the period of the vision statement. VISION CSFs force you to think beyond operational issues to the big picture strategies that will contribute to bring your whole personal strategy into reality

So, be clear about what a vision is and is not. Dream big dreams and 'listen' to your dreams. Write your vision statement in the personal strategy workbook. Then write VISION CSFs to support your vision.

While your vision statement is a very clear statement – SMART – of a desired future state, your VISION CSFs allow you some latitude and scope to be more general. Be definite about your vision but allow some flexibility in how you get there.

Dreaming big dreams requires you to be, to do, to have, to give as follows:

"To Be"
- Confident within yourself
- Who you are, different, purposeful, vulnerable
- True to yourself, responsible, courageous
- Happy, healthy, wealthy.

"To Do"
- Activities that are consistent with your values, mission, vision and goals
- What you do, with pride and integrity
- More than you get paid for, to go that extra mile without expecting a return
- Nothing sometimes and be at peace with the silence.

"To Have"
- Reality checks, regularly
- Courage to confront, experiment, and have fun
- Operational and financial acumen in pursuit of your strategy
- Balance in all things.

"To Give"
- Up the need to be right
- Value, love, respect
- Something for nothing
- Thanks to God.

Now, for the next rubicon step ➡

RUBICON STEP 6

Writing Clear Strategic Goals ... The How

RUBICON STEP 1
CURRENT SITUATION ANALYSIS

RUBICON STEP 2
REVIEWING YOUR HISTORY

RUBICON STEP 3
CLARIFYING & ORDERING VALUES

RUBICON STEP 4
CRYSTALLISING YOUR MISSION

RUBICON STEP 5
COMMITTING TO A CLEAR VISION

RUBICON STEP 6
WRITING CLEAR STRATEGIC GOALS

RUBICON STEP 7
TACTICAL PLANNING & IMPLEMENTATION

"When you SET a goal as part of your strategy, you automatically register it into your subconscious mind which then takes on a power of its own and moves you towards the achievement of that goal"

RUBICON STEP 6: WRITING CLEAR STRATEGIC GOALS ... THE HOW

Crossing the rubicon is a metaphor for taking bold and decisive action in your life and strategic success is measured, ultimately, as the progressive realisation of your predetermined goals. Therefore, your ability to set and achieve clearly defined goals is the ultimate successful outcome of all personal and professional life. While your vision is your BIG goal – your major definite purpose – your strategic goals give operational purpose to this vision. It's vital that you are clear about the difference between *setting* goals and *achieving* goals.

Setting goals is a systematic, written, methodology. Achieving things is automatic, if you just get out of your bed and do a decent days work every day. If you have no goals SET, how can you ACHIEVE them? If you have no goals set any road will get you there. The difference is as night is to day. If you don't comprehend this point you have missed the message of strategy formulation.

You should have 6-10 strategic goals for your personal and professional life. Each strategic goal should be achievable within a 24-month timeframe. Mini-goals that can be completed within 3-6-12 months are probably tasks or tactical plans, not strategic goals.

Each goal should be SMART, that is **S**pecific, **M**easurable, **A**chievable, **R**esults-oriented and **T**ime-bounded. You must be able to say 'Yes/No', 'I did/did not' achieve the goal at the end of the defined period. There must be no lack of clarity and you must put metrics on it. You can measure time, money and progress but not sentiments. Good intentions are not strategy. Hope is not a goal.

BEST PRACTICE GOAL SETTING

Goal setting can transform your life from ordinary to extraordinary. However, you must follow best practice principles or guidelines as follows:

i. **Harmonious And Consistent Goals:** Your values, mission and vision must be consistent with your goals. Your values represent your deepest convictions and your mission crystallises your purpose in life. Your vision is your big goal. When all three elements are in harmony, you dramatically increase the firepower of your goals.

Contradictory goals 'bump into' each other and cause you inner conflict and stress. For example, family time and career progression can frequently clash. Female executives in one fast growth company, who were mothers, felt they were looked on unfavourably for promotion because they had to forgo evenings out with their team. Trade-offs are inevitable and companies as well as individuals need to consider this.

ii. **Synchronise Your Talents With Your Goals:** Talents come in two major forms. First, are the more technical, functional, threshold talents that can be turned into sharp-end competencies by learning, education, up-skilling and practice. These are often entry level competencies into a job or career but, in the long term, only contribute about 20 percent impact to your success.

Second, are the more inborn attributes, traits and 'being' talents that need to be cultivated just as much to turn you into a leader. Leaders are made, not born. Unfortunately, these are the neglected talents and, consequently, the majority of individuals suffer most of their pain in this area.

Goal setting and development provides a platform to cater for both dimensions. In other words, find ways to embed the needs you have to develop in your goal setting in both dimensions of your talents.

iii. **Hard Work, Luck, Opportunity And Goal Achieving:** The golfing legend, Arnold Palmer, immortalised these words "The harder I practice the luckier I get". There is no substitute for hard work toward the achievement of your goals, but the law of averages seems to make "fortune favour the bold". The more things you try, the luckier you get. Probability and luck go hand in hand. The likelihood of winning anything is dramatically increased by the number of chances you take.

iv. **Variety Is The Spice Of Goal Setting:** There is no amount of success at work that can compensate for unhappiness at home. Therefore, your goals need to incorporate all the aspects of your life. There needs to be personal goals to serve your own needs and wants (e.g. personal development, health, hobbies). Family goals can be centred around children and your spouse (e.g. holidays, sport). Professional goals serve your career needs (e.g. qualifications, promotion).

Business goals can focus on commercial realities (e.g. revenue targets, production outputs). Financial goals could be another dimension. Community is another. Balance is the key, not all one dimension to the detriment of another area. A goal should stretch you to achieve it. An activity that you do daily is not a goal. It's an activity or a 'to-do' but not a goal.

CLARITY AND FOCUS REGARDING STRATEGY AND GOAL SETTING

Strategic masters realise there are two parts to excellent strategy. The first is strategy formulation and the second is strategy execution. While the whole is greater than the sum of its parts, writing your personal strategy 'goes live' with goal setting.

Your current situation analysis (rubicon step 1) was just that, information gathering, analysis and assessment. The history review (rubicon step 2) should help with perspective, identify patterns and thought processes.

Values and mission (rubicon steps 3 & 4) helped clarify how you want to be for the future. The Vision (rubicon step 5) 'forced your hand' to make a clear, decisive statement about where you want to be in practical terms in about five years.

Strategic goal setting (rubicon steps 6 & 7) is the master craft of strategy formulation. Goal achievement is the master expertise of strategy execution or implementation, which has been, sublimely, taking shape from the very start of this process.

Goal setting takes courage because it challenges your thinking and then your actions to move out of your natural comfort zone. It's this comfort zone that turns most people into 'wandering generalities rather than meaningful specifics'.

A well formulated overall strategy executed badly, at the implementation stage, will fail. An average strategy, executed well, can achieve outstanding success. It follows that a well formulated and a well executed strategy is **the** essential mixture necessary to cross your own rubicon. Once this formulation stage is completed, your strategic goals become the main focus for your operational actions throughout the year. When you ask the question 'What is the best use of my time today, this week, this month, this year?' the answer, invariably, should be: 'Concentrate on moving forward on one of my strategic goals.'

Your ability to 'stay strategic' over an extended period of time is a mental discipline that few people have mastered. Some find it difficult to 'stay strategic' even for a few hours. Some can't stay focused for even 30 minutes. Here is another focus question to engrave on your desk 'Is what I am doing right now helping to push forward one of my strategic goals?' If the answer is 'No' you may need to rethink.

Remember, discipline is doing the thing you have to do, when you have to do it, whether you feel like doing it or not. The bottom line is that crossing your personal or professional rubicon is a discipline. Determination and persistence are important. Self-discipline is how these fine qualities are best manifested. Clarity and focus help give you the discipline, determination and desire to make it happen.

Strategic goals are important, but rarely urgent. "Our greatest danger in life is in permitting the urgent things to crowd out the important" is how significant Charles Hummel, the philosopher, viewed it. Your strategic goals help keep the important top of mind for a greater time period.

Goal achieving may involve learning to delegate, research and development, outsourcing, arranging finance, re-deploying some of your six resources or a re-engineering of your lifestyle. Finding a space at home to call your own office or thinking space helps this process.

Goal achieving also involves character tests. Conviction and faith are imperatives. Focus and concentration moves you toward the accomplishment of your goals more rapidly than any other factor. Thomas Mann said that "Order and simplification are the first steps towards the mastery of a subject". Gandhi worked on the principle that "Action expresses priorities".

Your strategic goals should incorporate your driving forces and core competencies. These are the collective knowledge and skills that make you different. They are what you are really good at, your talents. Could your know-how (intellectual property) be used in another way? Is it properly positioned right now?

Here is an example of the strategic goals of a manager whose VISION 2011 is "To create a net worth of €3 million by 2011". Her VISION CSFs to support her VISION 2011 were: sales management competencies, develop relationships with three professional advisors, systematic networking, financial literacy, travel, reading and community. She wrote up these CSFs as shown earlier.

She has developed six strategic goals as follows:

i. **Career:** To get promoted to the role of Sales Director and work out a performance-related pay deal with my employer that would generate income of €150-250k per annum by 8th March 2008.

ii. **Investments:** To invest €1,000,000 in four properties with 90 percent rental income to offset my repayments by 8th September 2009.

iii. **Professional:** To complete 100 hours of formal professional development per year (average of one day per month) as available in the company.

iv. **Health/Sport:** To stay fit (run 50 miles on average per week) by training to run in one major marathon per year in London, New York and Paris (next three years).

v. **Family:** To spend 20 days on holiday including three long (four-day) weekends away with my family (scheduled in Jan-March).

vi. **Home:** To landscape the garden and build an extension to our family home not to exceed €300k by 30th June 2008.

Another example is a business owner whose vision is "To grow the value of my business by three times to €20 million and prepare an exit strategy plan which allows a management buy in or trade sale by 10th December 2011".

His critical success factors to support his VISION 2011 were centered around seven VISION CSF areas: Key account management, a family succession plan, production excellence, acquiring the business of a competitor, building a strong management team, a personal investment strategy and playing golf to single figure handicap level (to keep fit).

His 24 month strategic goals are:

i. **Production:** Install a state of the art production facility with a €900,000 investment by 21st April 2008.

ii. **Talent:** Hire a new production manager with the big time experience to set up a top class factory by 15th May 2007.

iii. **Customers:** To acquire two key customers of €3-6 million each by 20th December 2008.

iv. **Wealth:** To build personal assets to €6 million by 20th December 2009.

v. **Home:** To move house to the country by 10th October 2008.

vi. **Management:** To complete an MBA course to help develop my leadership skill by 4th May 2007.

Notice that each goal is just a SMART statement of a desired future state. The details come later. Each goal can be a project in itself. The natural tendency to 'argue' with HOW each goal can or cannot be achieved must be resisted at this point. Just set them down for now, using the SMART parameters and the best practice goal setting principles.

You'll be amazed at how much 'How Power' you will have later ... and creativity ... and innovation ... and team spirit ... and focus. But now you have a thinking process and a planning framework to make sense of it. Emotional strategy in action. The tactics, (rubicon step 7) at last, give that real 'hands-on' planning feel.

Now, for the next rubicon step ➡

RUBICON STEP 7

Tactical Planning & Implementation ... The When

| RUBICON STEP 1 |
| CURRENT SITUATION ANALYSIS |

| RUBICON STEP 2 |
| REVIEWING YOUR HISTORY |

| RUBICON STEP 3 |
| CLARIFYING & ORDERING VALUES |

| RUBICON STEP 4 |
| CRYSTALLISING YOUR MISSION |

| RUBICON STEP 5 |
| COMMITTING TO A CLEAR VISION |

| RUBICON STEP 6 |
| WRITING CLEAR STRATEGIC GOALS |

| RUBICON STEP 7 |
| **TACTICAL PLANNING & IMPLEMENTATION** |

"Think on paper ... Failing to plan is planning to fail ... Clarity, focus and execution are the essence of good tactics"

RUBICON STEP 7: TACTICAL PLANNING & IMPLEMENTATION ... THE WHEN

Tactical plans are the operational plans and tasks that are necessary to carry out each strategic goal. They are, in effect, short-term goals. They must be SMART in how they are written or follow a project management system. Otherwise, they are just nice ideas or well intentioned statements.

'*Who does what?*' and '*By when?*' are key questions in tactical business planning. Even in a personal situation, however, you can outsource, delegate responsibility to advisors, use other people's money, work with a partner, leverage time or expertise. These tactical plans become time management priorities but, as you can see now, they are time priorities with a purpose and within a context. In other words, you are working to a master plan, not a slave to a to-do list.

All strategic goals and tactical plans are designed to work towards the achievement of your vision, while being congruent with your values and mission. The whole is always greater than the sum of its parts. Harmonious consistency within all seven elements of the rubicon model acts as and 'energiser' in itself. Working harder is not stressful. Long work hours are like play hours and you have check points to help you cater for all the aspects of your life. The definition of a fanatic is 'someone who speeds up when they have lost sight of their goal (or have no goal)'. So, on the spectrum of day to day activity, move from being a fanatic to being a strategist.

At the end of each year, you should review and upgrade your strategic goals and re-focus on your vision, mission and core values. Sit down with your significant-other or family and compare notes and progress. The most powerful partnership on earth is a couple who *cross the rubicon* together and share/support each other's plans and ambitions. Adjust as necessary. Nothing is carved in marble, keep your options open. Be clear and strong about your vision and goals, but be flexible in terms of how you achieve those targets, because obstacles will occur and crises will inevitably happen as part of life's journey.

Your values and mission, however, should not change in any significant way over time. Your vision statements will change over the years but your strategic goals should be upgraded every twelve to twenty-four months or even more regularly. As necessary, tactical plans should be constantly changed, upgraded, completed or eliminated. They are a '*living thing*.'

General George Patton (1885-1945), one of the most colourful American Generals of World War II, said: 'No plan ever survives contact with the enemy.' In personal strategic thinking and planning, there is a constant evolution and movement. So be flexible. Make a mess of your rubicon document when you have written it. I have seen tattered well-inked rubicons two-to-four years later. I have seen couples hold on to their copy like a child holds a favourite toy. A messy well-worked document is surely better than a beautifully produced unused plan!

Finally, remember not to confuse tasks and activities with strategic goals or tactical plans. Everyone completes tasks and activities every day and this mode of living may very well move you forward over time. For example, driving home this evening or completing a report by 4.00pm are not goals ... these are activities. Hundreds, even thousands of small activities, tasks or projects contribute to your achieving the goals you have set, but they are just that, activities for your to-do list or tasks to be completed. They do help you progressively work towards the vision and strategic goals that you have set. Achieving the goals you have SET is a proactive systematic process and puts you in charge of your destiny, rather than letting circumstances dictate your life.

On the next page there is an example of a strategic goal – career development – with full tactical plans written up. The beauty of this, one page, strategic goal is simplicity, clarity and focus in action.

Strategic Goal One: CAREER DEVELOPMENT

EXAMPLE

THE GOAL: To get promoted to the position of Financial Director (FD) and get invited to join the main board of the company by 10th January 2009.

Tactical Plan One: Project Ulysses
To bring home project Ulysses on time and on budget to demonstrate that I can competently handle a major project. (This project can transform 'how we do business').

20th Sept 2007

Tactical Plan Two: MBA
To complete my part time MBA and clear the decks to concentrate on developing my career. (To do taxation exams in the next three months).

4th Dec 2008

Tactical Plan Three: Build Department
To hire a No. 2 Accountant and delegate all operational procedures to him/her. To build the department into a strong team of 12 people with a strong customer support ethos in the company.

30th June 2007

Tactical Plan Four: Board Members
To network with all six of the current board on a personal basis. Invite to dinner in my home. (Get involved with individuals as necessary. Build relationships).

By mid-year

Tactical Plan Five: Presentations
To practice and learn professional presentation skills. Take a course. Find opportunities to speak at two conferences to increase my profile outside the company and to gain confidence. To represent the company in public.

4th Nov 2007

Tactical Plan Six: Networking
To join the Association of Financial Controllers and get on the committee at the next AGM. (The objective is to 'stay current' and alert to trends and innovation in accounting).

April 2008

Tactical Plan Seven: Internal Marketing
To broaden my horizons on production and marketing. Have lunch each quarter with Production Director and Marketing Director. To actively bring solutions to their problems. To be seen as more than just the accountant. To visit key customers.

Ongoing

Cross-check this goal with your overall strategy: 1. Is this goal SMART and following the best practice goal setting principles? 2. Does this goal take account of history patterns and emerging points from your CSA? (Current Situation Analysis Step 1) 3. Is this goal consistent with your values, mission and vision statements? (Steps 3, 4 & 5) 4. Does this goal put operational wheels on your dreams and vision CSFs to achieve your vision? (Step 5) 5. Will this goal move you significantly forward over the next two years? 6. Is this consistent with your time management priorities, projects, tasks and to-do list?

THE FINAL CHECK

EIGHT FUNDAMENTAL STRATEGY PRINCIPLES

THE FINAL CHECK: EIGHT FUNDAMENTAL STRATEGY PRINCIPLES

How do you put your personal strategy to the test against fundamental strategic principles? Before you put the final touches to completing your rubicon strategy, run a check using the **OOMMEEES** screening system. OOMMEEES is an acronym which comprises the eight basic principles of all good business strategy: **O**bjective, **O**ffensive, **M**ass, **M**anoeuvre, **E**conomy, **E**xploitation, **E**xecution, **S**urprise.

All good-to-great business or personal strategy has parallels in military strategy. Each of the OOMMEEES elements can be present to a greater or lesser degree in your final document. It should be used like a filtering system to establish the overall strength of your strategic framework.

Each letter in the OOMMEEES formula represents a key strategic principle:

- The Principle of **Objective:** Is there absolute clarity and focus in your overall objective?

- The Principle of **Offensive:** Is your strategy action-oriented?

- The Principle of **Mass:** Has it power and purpose?

- The Principle of **Manoeuvre:** How flexible is your strategy and how quickly could you change?

- The Principle of **Economy:** Could you be wasting resources on secondary objectives?

- The Principle of **Exploitation:** Are you maximising all your talents and potential?

- The Principle of **Execution:** Are you relentlessly living the strategy? Making it happen? Implementing the goals.

- The Principle of **Surprise:** Do you carefully plan and execute your strategy with a sense of urgency?

When you have reviewed this section and completed your write up, go back through your personal strategy and cross-check the fundamentals: What emerged from your current situation analysis? What patterns emerged from your history? Are your values and mission evident in the goal-setting stages? Are your VISION CSFs the bridge between your vision and your strategic goals?

Then go through each strategy principle on the following pages:

FUNDAMENTAL STRATEGIC PRINCIPLES

<u>O</u>OMMEEES
↑

i. **DEFINITION OF THE PRINCIPLE OF THE OBJECTIVE**

Focus all your personal and professional efforts in the direction of an overall, major, SMART objective.

CLARITY OF OBJECTIVE: KNOW WHAT YOU WANT

All good strategy must have a well-defined, clear objective. The principle of the objective requires clear thinking on your values, mission and vision of your personal business. Commitment and clarity about the overall strategy process is an essential step towards achieving the clear objective.

You must sell the overall objective to yourself first! You must explain to those close to you what you have created and give insights into 'the How'. If your family have enough reasons (Know-Why), they will overcome any How.

The purpose of rubicon strategy is the achievement of your vision and the fulfilment of your life's mission, whilst being consistent with your values.

CRITICAL QUESTIONS FOR FOCUS AND CONCENTRATION

1. Have you absolute clarity about what you are trying to achieve?
2. Will your family support you and take collective responsibility for the strategic implementation?
3. Will the implementation of your strategy differentiate you from your colleagues?
4. Do you have a routine to avoid distractions to make this happen?

5. Do you have 'a place' to concentrate on this strategy?
6. What are your assumptions?
7. What would happen if your assumptions are wrong?

What The Great Leaders Have Said About Objective

"A personal computer for every person, on every desk — Bill Gates

"If you don't have a strategy you will be ... part of somebody else's strategy"
— Toffler

"Pursue one great decisive aim with force and determination"
— Karl Von Clausewitz

"Proceed to London. Invade Europe. Defeat the Germans"
— General Dwight D. Eisenhower, 1941

"Get the Iraqis out of Kuwait"— General Norman Schwarzkopf, 1991

"To be certain to take what you attack is to attack a place the enemy does not protect" — Sun Tzu

"Errant assumptions lie at the root of every failure" — MacKenzie

"Success doesn't mean the absence of failures; it means the attainment of ultimate objectives" – Edwin Bliss

"Failure comes only when we forget our ideals and objectives and principles"
— Jawaharlal Nehru

"The care of human life and happiness, and not their destruction, is the first and only object of good government" — Thomas Jefferson

An Example Of The Principle Of Objective

A 24 year old had an obsession about owning property. He worked night and day for two years, saving every penny for the deposit on his first house. He rented it out and leveraged it to buy a second and a third house. By 30 years of age, his goal was to have six houses. Today, he is 30 years old and he has ten houses. He has now refocused on another magnificent objective by the time he is 40.

FUNDAMENTAL STRATEGIC PRINCIPLES
O**O**MMEEES
   ↑

ii. **DEFINITION OF THE PRINCIPLE OF THE OFFENSIVE**

Taking and keeping the initiative with audacity and purposeful actions.

THE PRINCIPLE OF THE CONTINUOUS OFFENSIVE

An essential principle of all good strategy is the act of taking the offensive, and moving forward. So consider your forward momentum. Get going. Develop a bias for action. Remember, you only have to succeed the last time.

The flip-side of the offensive principle, ironically, is the military principle of security. (For example, building a financial fortress around your private life requires thought and sacrifice). All serious money is patient money. Build your run rate. It means taking nothing for granted. It means protecting yourself against setbacks (e.g. like confusing employment with employability). Short-term pain means long-term gain in most cases. Offensive and security go hand-in-hand.

Courage is one mark of personal leadership, and courage is always expressed in a willingness to go forward. Robert Green said "When in doubt, act audaciously. Audacity will get you in trouble now and then, but even more audacity will usually get you out".

CRITICAL QUESTIONS FOR FOCUS AND CONCENTRATION

1. What new initiatives does your strategic framework take?
2. Is your personal and professional offensive moving in the right direction, and aligned?

3. Will the implementation of this strategy give you a significant competitive edge?

4. Is it an action-oriented strategy?

5. Will it allow you to market 'the difference' and build your personal brand, to your audience?

6. Are you continuously networking, growing, acquiring, gaining momentum?

7. Regarding security, what is the worst possible outcome here?

WHAT THE GREAT LEADERS HAVE SAID ABOUT OFFENSIVE

"No great battles are ever won on the defensive" — Napoleon

"It's impossible to be too strong at the decisive point" — Napoleon

"Never pay for the same ground twice" — Patton (in terms of men and material)

"War, once declared, must be waged offensively, aggressively" — Mahan

"Opportunities? I make opportunities" — Napoleon

"Courage is resistance to fear, mastery of fear — not absence of fear"
— Mark Twain

"We make war that we may live in peace" — Aristotle

"There never was a good war or a bad peace" — Benjamin Franklin

"There is nothing so likely to produce peace as to be well prepared to meet the enemy" — George Washington

OFFENSIVE EXAMPLES

Joe decided to ASK his way to success. He wrote down the names of 10 influencers who could help him with knowledge, money and time. Three were business leaders, three were family and four were total strangers. He emailed, phoned and wrote to all ten and got all kinds of introductions and 'offensive' ideas. He explained some ideas he had to start a business and asked for any advise or help these people could give him. He was overwhelmed with the responses including one investor who took 30 percent equity in his new enterprise.

FUNDAMENTAL STRATEGIC PRINCIPLES

OO**M**MEEES
   ↑

iii. DEFINITION OF **THE PRINCIPLE OF MASS**

Focus and concentration, with purpose and power, at the right place and time.

MASSING YOUR RESOURCES

When considering critical mass, intensity of purpose and massed concentration are vital to strategic thinking and planning. Lack of concentration and focus are major human failings. Distraction is everywhere. Discipline fades. Persistence withers. You must do what you committed to do with the right force to create personal and professional strategic advantage.

Clear communication at home is a critical factor in concentration. Finding a place and a routine is vital. At work, mobilising the technical driving forces/resources and the human magnificent obsession together is the essence of mass.

Quality time and attention at home, and sales and profitability at work, are the imperatives for strategic success. Your ability to concentrate on a work life balance is the critical success factor. Cost management, with top-line sales success deliver the bottom-line profits at work, but an equal concentration on the affairs of home life is imperative.

CRITICAL QUESTIONS FOR FOCUS AND CONCENTRATION

1. Have you considered how you bring about superior scale in critical resource areas at the right time, in the right place, with the right impact?

2. How do you mass your resources with your thinking and planning process/framework to gain a decisive edge?
3. Is there a concentration of effort, time and money on your basic business competencies?
4. What's your choke point? What's stopping you? Why are you not there already?
5. How could you leverage help? Who could assist?
6. How is your marketing offensive with regard to specialisation, differentiation, segmentation, concentration and positioning?
7. What one critical success factor (sales, leadership), if you developed and executed it in an excellent way, would dramatically help you achieve your vision and strategic goals.

WHAT THE GREAT LEADERS HAVE SAID ABOUT MASSING YOUR RESOURCES

"Wherever you see something big getting done, you'll find a monomaniac in there somewhere" — Peter Drucker

"The will to conquer is the first condition of victory"— F. Foch

"Most misfortunes are the result of misused time"— Napoleon Hill

"Don't try to be all things. Pick a few things to be good at and be the best you can" — Liz Ashe

"Chance only favours the mind that is prepared" — Louis Pasteur

"It is an unfortunate fact that we can secure peace only by preparing for war"
— John F. Kennedy

"There are no warlike people, just warlike leaders" — Ralph Bunche

MASS EXAMPLES

Mary focused all her time and attention on selling one product to one niche market in excellent fashion. She is now regarded as 'the expert' in her field as a consultant and advisor to her clients. She is a problem-solver and a value-adder, and earns triple the income of the average performer in her field. She is a product knowledge 'guru' and the obvious expert on her subject in her industry. Her talent and competency set is in developing peer level relationships with 'ideal customers' in a few niche markets.

FUNDAMENTAL STRATEGIC PRINCIPLES

OOM<u>M</u>EEES
⬆

iv. DEFINITION OF **THE PRINCIPLE OF MANOEUVRE**

The ability to adjust the plan to actual circumstances and to search for a way to find alternative means of victory when necessary.

MANOEUVRE AS AN OPTION

You must be flexible and mobile with your resources to deal with any likely threats and exploit emerging opportunities. Change dictates this. In military terms, deviation, deception or the indirect approach are regarded as excellent tactics. Learn to become a moving target. Adapt, adjust, be flexible.

Be clear about your objective, but be <u>flexible</u> about how you achieve it.

The critical variable with manoeuvre/mobility is people. 'Good people are free' because they are nett contributors to the bottom line. If unfounded or false expectations are raised it can often lead to a cynical back-lash to the overall strategic process. The resource that will cause you the most problems will be the people resource. Manage people extra carefully. The bottom line is this: 'If you help enough people achieve what they want, you will achieve what you want'.

Failure to anticipate, failure to learn, and failure to adapt are the three primary reasons for military defeat according to experts. Don't they apply also to your personal and professional strategy?

CRITICAL QUESTIONS FOR FOCUS AND CONCENTRATION
1. How flexible and how quickly can you react to change?
2. Could you move the necessary resources into place and re-deploy hitherto under-utilised resources to exploit opportunities?
3. Knowing what you now know about … would you still … ?
4. What manoeuvres are you/should you be scheming?

5. How are you managing your time and money to achieve your overall objective?
6. How do you deploy your brain power with regard to innovation and continuous betterment?
7. Are you mobile and flexible enough to re-allocate resources to exploit unexpected success or reduce sudden vulnerability?
8. How good is your intelligence gathering? Is your 'intelligence' or feedback (control) system capable of giving early warning signals?
9. Have you a Bismarck plan — a 'plan B'?
10. Are you thinking outside the box or are you falling in love with your own ideas?

WHAT THE GREAT LEADERS HAVE SAID ABOUT MANOEUVRE

"No strategy ever survives first contact with the enemy" — Patton

"The more you do of what you are doing, the more you will get of what you've got" — Anonymous

"Whatever got you to where you are today is not enough to keep you there"

"We don't mind if people make mistakes. This is normal and natural. What is unforgivable is the failure to learn from the mistakes" — Watson, IBM

"In baiting a mousetrap with cheese, always leave room for the mouse" — Saki

"No more prizes for predicting rain. Prizes only for building arks"
— Anonymous

"While technically I did not commit a crime, an impeachable offence … these are legalisms, as far as the handling of this matter is concerned' it was so botched up, I made so many bad judgments. The worst ones, mistakes of the heart, rather than the head. But let me say, a man in that top job – he's got to have a heart, but his head must always rule his heart"
— Richard Milhous Nixon

MANOEUVRE EXAMPLES

Steve Jobs (Apple) vs. Bill Gates' (Microsoft) view of personal computing and operating systems.
Schwarzkopf's 1991 'Hail Mary' manoeuvre in the Iraqi war.
Alexander the Great's manoeuvre against Darius of Persia in the battle of Gaugamela, where 35,000 soldiers routed 400,000.

FUNDAMENTAL STRATEGIC PRINCIPLES

OOMM<u>E</u>EES
⬆

v. DEFINITION OF **THE PRINCIPLE OF ECONOMY**

Critical resources are always scarce and must be conserved to mass them in the most efficient and effective manner to achieve the primary objective.

ECONOMY OF RESOURCE DEPLOYMENT

A principle of economics is that critical resources — time, money, talent, product — are always scarce. Your ability to achieve your vision and strategic goals at the lowest possible cost is essential to strategy success. A financial measure is the easiest to calculate but it's not the only cost.

We would all have a better chance to achieve our victories if we had limitless resources. The secret of good strategy, however, is to use your available resources sparingly and to secure your position so as to protect your resources from counter moves, or for the 'rainy day'. Crisis anticipation is important here.

You can make great things happen if you invest a small fortune in it. However, many of the best strategic initiatives cost very little money, but they require an investment cost of thinking time. For example, wise long-term investments and/or a passive income stream are two ways to leverage your time and money. Be prudent. Be wise. Learn to save and invest.

CRITICAL QUESTIONS FOR FOCUS AND CONCENTRATION

1. How much will this initiative cost you across all resources?
2. How can you deploy your resources and implement your strategy at the least cost?
3. Have you costed and budgeted your plans (cash flow projection, etc.)?
4. Have you budgeted to achieve the objectives with minimum expenditure?
5. What core competencies could you use to double your impact?

6. Are you wasting resources on secondary objectives?
7. What is your appreciation of wealth management and financial independence?
8. Do you know your 'time to payback'?
9. What is your financial run rate?

WHAT THE GREAT LEADERS HAVE SAID ABOUT ECONOMY

"Never yield ground. It is cheaper to hold what you have than to re-take what you have lost" — Patton

"Make money slowly" — Stanley and Danko

"Pay yourself first" — George Glasson

"Expenses rise to meet income" — C. Northcote Parkinson

"Early to bed and early to rise help make a person healthy, wealthy and wise".
— Benjamin Franklin

"Beware of little expenses; a small leak will sink a great ship"
— Benjamin Franklin

"The man who will live above his present circumstances, is in great danger of soon living beneath them" — Joseph Addison

"Without economy none can be rich, and with it few will be poor" – Samuel Johnson

"He who will not economise will have to agonise" - Confucius

ECONOMY EXAMPLES

One of the reasons that Wellington won the Battle of Waterloo was because he held back 17,000 troops for a 'what if' scenario. His decision was central to winning one of the greatest military battles of all time.

In 200 BC a Greek, General Pyrrhic, had just won a battle and was being congratulated for his success. "Alas" he said "one more such victory and I am undone". Although he won the battle his losses were terrible. His comment gave rise to the term '*pyrrhic victory*'. Remember, "absolute" resource loss cannot be made up in time or purchase.

FUNDAMENTAL STRATEGIC PRINCIPLES
OOMME*E*S
↑

vi. DEFINITION OF **THE PRINCIPLE OF EXPLOITATION**

Taking advantage of a success by vigorously following through to maximise the total potential of an opportunity.

EXPLOITATION OF OPPORTUNITIES, DEFENSE OF WEAKNESSES

Exploitation means having the 'killer instinct'. It means follow-up and follow-through. Going all the way to the objective. Relentlessly. Never slowing down. In business it means keeping your competitors off-balance.

When you've got a clear direction and you are focused on the outcome, your next vital step is to implement and exploit all the opportunities available to you. The fear of taking risks, self-limiting beliefs, procrastination, lack of focus and direction will be your main internal causes of strategy failure. In battle, you would strike at your competitors' *Achilles Heel* and exploit their weaknesses. That is, to focus on your strong points and their weak points for success. (An alternative strategy is to attack their strength).

CRITICAL QUESTIONS FOR FOCUS AND CONCENTRATION

1. Are you researching and watching out for new trends and emerging opportunities in your industry and gearing up to exploit them if they are consistent with your overall strategic thrust?
2. Do these trends or opportunities build on or complement your strengths?
3. What and where is your Achilles Heel?
4. Does your offering do what you say it will do?
5. Do your customers value 'the edge' you offer them? Do you consider your boss as a customer?

6. How can you exploit your edge even more?
7. Could your *'Acres of Diamonds'* lie close at hand?
8. How much value/weight does your personal brand carry?
9. How can you leverage yourself in a significantly better way?

WHAT THE GREAT LEADERS HAVE SAID ABOUT EXPLOITATION

"On the plains of hesitation lie the bleached bones of countless millions, who at the dawn of victory, sat down to wait, and waiting, lost all."

"Opportunities are like windows — they open and close quite quickly. Take immediate action if the opportunity supports your objectives"

"Under capitalism, man exploits man. Under communism, it's just the opposite" – John Kenneth Galbraith

"Exploitation and oppression is not a matter of race. It is the system, the apparatus of world-wide brigandage called imperialism, which made the Powers behave the way they did" – Han Suyin

"The human race cannot forever exist half-exploiters and half-exploited"

– Henry Ford

"The law was made for one thing alone, for the exploitation of those who don't understand it" – Bertolt Brecht

EXPLOITATION EXAMPLES

Swiss watch-makers first designed a quartz watch in 1960 but failed to exploit its potential and it effectively devastated their industry from 60,000 to 12,000 workers in a decade. The Japanese exploited the digital watch market for a 'mere' royalty.

The German army of 3,000,000 failed to follow through on the invasion of Russia in WWII and effectively lost the initiative and the war over that decision.

Desert Storm (1991) is a good example of not exploiting an initial success in Iraq. Thirteen years later, Allied troops went all the way to Baghdad and destroyed the Saddam Hussein dictatorship.

FUNDAMENTAL STRATEGIC PRINCIPLES
OOMMEE<u>E</u>S
↑

vii. **DEFINITION OF THE PRINCIPLE OF EXECUTION**
To reach your objectives by clear, concise, concerted and direct action under your responsible leadership.

EXECUTION IS THE ULTIMATE TEST

Many a poor plan has been rescued by superb execution. Everything depends on execution. Having a vision is not the solution on its own. More importantly, many (theoretically) brilliant plans have been wrecked because some key resource (or person) was not put in place or because the plans were too complicated to understand, or because a competitor was allowed the opportunity to manoeuvre and take a counter-offensive. In the end, all strategy is action and execution oriented.

Diffusion of effort, complexity and confusion are the destroyers of military, business and personal endeavours. Concentrate all your 'execution force', therefore, on keeping it simple.

Commitment to implement your strategy is vital to success. Without commitment there is hesitation – the chance to hold back – and the result is always poor performance and stress. Commitment takes courage.

CRITICAL QUESTIONS FOR FOCUS AND CONCENTRATION
1. Can you think 'big picture' AND orchestrate operationally?
2. Have you got the strategic leadership competencies?
3. What are the critical multipliers that can fast-forward your results?

4. How do circumstances reveal your leadership strength in depth?
5. Who is the most indispensable person in terms of making your strategy happen?
6. Who are your advisors, confidants and mentors?
7. What is the simplest and most direct way to execute your strategy?

What The Great Leaders Have Said About Execution

"Everything should be made as simple as possible, but not simpler" — Einstein

"No one ever stops you from going the extra mile at work" — Napoleon Hill

"The strength of the wolf is the pack and the strength of the pack is the wolf"
— Rudyard Kipling

"When placed in command, take charge" — Napoleon

"The only inevitable event in the life of the leader is the recurring crisis"
— Peter Drucker

"Leadership is practiced not so much in words as in attitude and in actions" — Harold S. Geneen

"Don't be too timid and squeamish about your actions. All life is an experiment" — Ralph Waldo Emerson

"No enterprise is more likely to succeed than one concealed from the enemy until it is ripe for execution" — Niccolo Machiavelli

"It is easy enough to be friendly to one's friends. But to befriend the one who regards himself as your enemy is the quintessence of true religion. The other is mere business" – Mohandas K. Gandhi

"Even if you're on the right track, you'll get run over if you just sit there"
— Will Rogers

Execution Examples

Concerted action in the 2001 Afghanistan war destroyed the Taliban regime in less than six weeks. And a similar time in the 2003 Iraqi war.

In Fortune 500 companies the number one reason 28 CEOs were fired: "Failure to execute". — Lou Gerstner, IBM, 1993 turnaround.

FUNDAMENTAL STRATEGIC PRINCIPLES
OOMMEEE<u>S</u>
↑

viii. **DEFINITION OF THE PRINCIPLE OF SURPRISE**

To accomplish the purpose before the enemy can react effectively.
— *Westpoint*

THE SURPRISE VARIABLE: DO THE UNEXPECTED

One of the most powerful strategies in shifting the balance of combat in a war is the military principle of surprise. With surprise comes elements of deception, cover, effective intelligence and counter intelligence, variation in tactics and methods of operation.

In business today surprise is SPEED to market, SPEED to customer. Just-in-time. Real time. Now. In many cases this factor alone can transform your business position. If you could get your whole company to 'think fast' you could probably double your business within a relatively short time frame. In personal and professional strategy it means SENSE OF URGENCY and expediency.

How much originality, speed, added-value and uniqueness can you bring to your strategic plans? When, where, why and how you kick off your strategic initiatives can add greatly to the overall impact. In military battles, as in sport, and in business, a new approach or surprise methodology can be the secret of a successful outcome. With personal strategy, you have total control of your own destiny … with minimal complexity.

Peter Drucker says: "The purpose of a business is to satisfy customers". Learn to surprise your customers by mastering four levels of customer service … basic satisfaction, exceeding expectations, delighting your customers, and amazing them. Your customers are your boss, your partners, your advisors, your mentors and your stakeholders.

CRITICAL QUESTIONS FOR FOCUS AND CONCENTRATION

1. Have you thought out the launch time, place and style of any new initiatives?
2. Will your approach be direct or indirect?
3. Who knows about it?
4. Who needs to know about it?
5. What advantage can be gained by keeping it a surprise?
6. How can you serve your customers better and faster than in the past?
7. Who do you need to amaze?
8. How good are you in a crisis?

WHAT THE GREAT LEADERS HAVE SAID ABOUT SURPRISE

"To capture the baby tiger, you have to go into the other tiger's lair"
— Japanese military WWII

"Never attack where the enemy expects you to come" — Patton

"Time changes everything except something within us which is always surprised by change" – Thomas Hardy

"The real artists work is a surprise to himself" – Robert Henri

"If you do not expect the unexpected, you will not find it, for it is not to be reached by search or trail" – Heraclitus

"Never tell people how to do things. Tell them what to do and they will surprise you with their ingenuity" – George S. Patton

SURPRISE EXAMPLES

Domino's Pizza: Deliver in 30 minutes or no charge.
Pearl Harbour, 7th December, 1941.
The D-Day landing in Normandy was a great surprise for the German armies in 1944 and one from which they never recovered.
The Israeli-Arab 1967 six-day war was a brilliant example of speed and surprise.

MEET THE ENEMY

BEYOND STRATEGY FORMULATION TO STRATEGY EXECUTION

BEYOND STRATEGY FORMULATION TO STRATEGY EXECUTION: MEET THE ENEMY

All great strategy has two almost distinct parts. The first is strategy formulation which this process has been largely about and the second is strategy execution which is your primary responsibility from this stage forward.

A poorly formulated strategy, brilliantly executed, will probably succeed better than a top notch, professionally formulated, document poorly executed. In other words, once you have completed the formulation stage, everything depends on execution. Just having a strategy – no matter how well formulated – is a recipe for cynicism, sarcasm and failure if it is not implemented.

'Being strategic' means putting a rubicon context on all your operational activities from here forward.

Strategic thinking is synergetic, divergent, creative, process-focused and innovative. The purpose of strategic thinking is to discover novel, imaginative strategies which can re-write the rules of the competitive game in your favour, and to envision potential futures significantly different from the present.

Strategic planning is analytical, convergent, conventional, formal, goals and positioning oriented. The purpose of strategic planning is to operationalise the strategies developed through strategic thinking and to harden up the strategic thinking process

However, you are not yet over the final hurdle. Your biggest challenge with implementation of the strategies you have written up will not be lack of resources, or time, or intention, or money. You have met the enemy already ... it's yourself.

The tendency to self-sabotage your good work could be the single biggest obstacle you face as you prepare to implement. The 'chatter-box' in your head needs to be understood first before the doing or executing or implementing stage kicks in.

One of your values or goals or vision CSFs may have been personal development. Facing the fears and doing it anyway is the key. The difference between the coward and the man or woman of courage is that they are both afraid, but the courageous person acts in spite of that fear.

i. **MONITOR THE EXECUTION**

Monitoring your progress is an imperative if you find you are holding back or not living up to the promises you have made yourself. This can be done by evaluating your formulated results in the *Writing Your Personal Strategy* workbook. Be aware of resistance or "yes but ..." language in your assessment.

Monitoring your execution levels can be weekly, monthly, quarterly or year on year. Monitor as you deem you need to and to the degree you feel necessary. Success breeds success. Nothing succeeds like success, so use your own best judgment at all times.

Obstacles are an inevitable part of life and work and are sent to instruct, not obstruct. Problems and challenges are attracted to you as lessons or gifts which you must master before you are free to move to the next step. So, embrace those blockages as valuable lessons and always focus on the 'How'. HOW will you solve the problem to allow you move relentlessly towards the achievement of your overall strategy? HOW will you solve the problem? HOW will you prevail?

Crossing the rubicon was that bold act that Caesar took in 49 BC that made him say "The die is now cast, there is no going back, ever again". Writing your personal strategy casts the die for you but, remember, the journey goes on once you did the inevitable. Sometimes people feel success is in the act itself. No! *Crossing the rubicon* is a huge statement, a decisive, irrevocable action, but for Caesar it meant war and for you challenges of another kind – living your values and your purpose, focusing on your vision, achieving those goals.

On 10th November 1942, Winston Churchill addressed the House of Commons regarding the Battle of Egypt. His words were apt for strategy executions. He said "Now this is not the end. It is not even the beginning of the end. But it is, perhaps, the end of the beginning".

One thing is clear, you can never go back to the old ways of working operationally rather than strategically. Working day to day, week to week, you do ACHIEVE things and make progress, but not the things you have strategically SET. That's what separates the strategic thinkers and planners from the rest of those in the field. Working strategically you have purpose, clarity and focus. Working operationally you confuse activity with real progress, busyness with business, efficiency with effectiveness, urgent with important and the result is anxiety, stress and confusion.

A great motivator is a sense of 'felt-dissatisfaction' and you now know you cannot ever re-cross this rubicon again. You may have to cross other rubicon rivers and this success template will guide you.

ii. **MONITOR THE TIMEFRAMES**

A year is a wonderful time-frame to consider progress on your strategy execution. In a year, you could change your life, transform your career, learn to be a strategist and achieve significant goals. You work about 2000 hours in the average year out of a total of 8760 hours. You have lots of time. Think one year out, five years out, 10 years out, even 20 years. Taking a long-term perspective is a key strategic success factor. Invest in the future return on your effort, not the immediate payback. Delay gratification on the pleasures of today for the vision of tomorrow. That's strategy in action. Every time you put aside an hour to plan it will be paid back to you tenfold, even more, in the future.

A quarter – three months – is like one of the four seasons. Over 90 days, the world can change or you can change your world. Most companies today think and plan in quarterly units. Bill Gates says his business is only three months away from extinction at any time – at least that is how he plans. Working to a quarter by quarter time-frame allows you some flexibility to catch up for a soft month or deal with occasional 'noise in the system'. It's a concrete business-like deadline and time frame. Use it to think more strategically on a personal level.

A month is an operational time frame but with all the measures and alignment possibilities to the year that it must be used to best potential. You can live strategically during the 30 or so days of a month or you can get bogged down in 'to-do' lists, tasks and problems.

A strategist delegates, outsources, time manages and keeps asking the strategic question: "What is the best use of my time this hour/day/week/month?" Plan your work on a 10 month year … plan your life on a 12 month year.

A week, of course, is the time frame that brings reality to our home and work lives. Time is the currency of day to day affairs. Time control is a master skill that you need to bring into your life.

A day, an hour, a minute are all time management capsules. The psychology of time management – strategy – is as important as the techniques of time management – operational – in terms of getting the right things done. Setting priorities, learning to say 'no' to interruptions and disciplining yourself to do important tasks rather than the nice to do trivial jobs are just some of the time necessities you need to master to get time to be strategic.

EPILOGUE

Crossing the rubicon is a metaphor for transforming your current reality on to a path of future progress and prosperity.

Change is the only constant today and this personal strategy process is about bringing clarity and focus to your future direction.

This book is the master blueprint to the printed or electronic workbook where you can write up your thoughts/ideas following the formula outlined herein. The workbook is called ***Writing Your Personal Strategy: Formulating The Seven Strategy Steps From The Rubicon Model.***

'Any system is superior to no system' is a piece of advice I learned decades ago. The rubicon system can guide you and act as a mentor as you concentrate on creating personal and professional advantage.

Michaelangelo used the immortal Latin words "Ancora Imparo" which means "I am still learning" at the age of 87. Well, I am also still learning and would appreciate your feedback on this process when you have completed it.

Good Luck

John Butler
johnbutler@centurymanagement.ie
www.centurymanagement.ie

APPENDICES

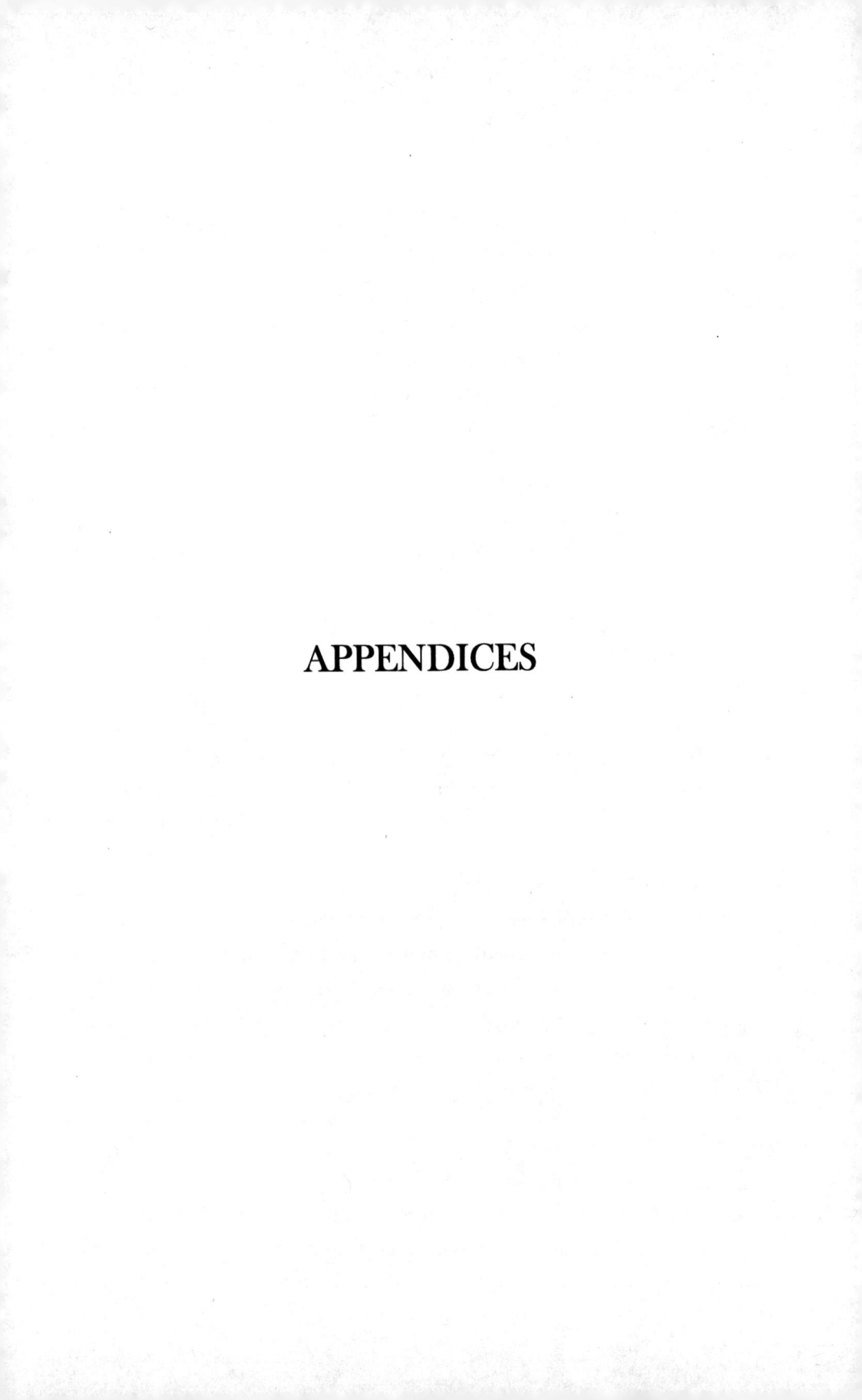

APPENDIX 1

IRELAND: CROSSING THE RUBICON AS A COUNTRY

Ireland as a country has *crossed the rubicon* as it stepped into the 21st century. What happened during the Celtic Tiger decade from 1996–2006 is a world class example of what a whole nation can do given the right circumstances.

The old war-cry was "Ireland long a province be a nation once again". The new war-cry is "Ireland long an economic basket case is a new, vibrant, dynamic, wealthy country".

Crossing the rubicon for Ireland sets a benchmark for every nation on earth and is fast becoming the model to study and copy. Here is a flavour of some of the *crossing the rubicon* transformations that took place in Ireland during the Celtic Tiger period:

- Productivity growth from 1995–2006 has been four times the European average according to the EU commission and wealth has grown 350 percent in the same period.
- Consumerism is the new religion born out of a credit liberalisation. Private debt to income is 130 percent.
- Social mobility is on the march with the middle class increasing by 25 percent. In a July 2006 survey of OECD nations, Ireland ranked second behind Japan and ahead of UK, US, Italy, France and Germany, showing an average wealth of nearly €150,000 per head of population.
- Education is flavour of the decade with a 40 percent increase in third level education and a 65 percent increase in PhDs in Ireland.
- Property investors we were, now we are global property speculators with Irish millionaires colonising the world.

NCB economists predict – via their report, *2020 Vision: Ireland's Demographic Dividend* – that by 2020 Ireland will have annual growth rates of five percent and a population of 5.3 million people of whom 20 percent will be immigrants. Is this blind faith or 20/20 vision or what you need to prepare for in your personal strategy formulation?

Crossing the rubicon is about coming to terms with *who you are* and *what you do* and making the necessary transformation from the old to the new. An individual, a company and a country – Ireland – can also *cross the rubicon* by following the same formula. Consider the *who we are/were* and *what we do/did* equation below:

THE NEW 21st CENTURY IRELAND

Who We Are Now

Ireland has crossed the rubicon. We are happy, self-confident and wealthy. In European and International surveys of best places to live, happiness indices and economic wellbeing, we rank as number one or very high. The Irish dream is being lived out and expectation and optimism levels are incredible. We have embraced the capitalist and wealth creation ethos. We are proud and ready to take our place among the nations of the world. We are future focused and thinking about tomorrow rather than yesterday. Since 2000, more than 750,000 immigrants have flown into Ireland from over 200 countries. Already, estimates are that up to 10 percent of the resident population are now foreign born. Ireland is a good place to come to and we are virtually at 100 percent employment.

What We Do Now

Productivity in Ireland is nearly four times the EU average over the period 1995–2005 according to the EU Commission. So, while we are prepared to work harder and commute longer hours than the rest of Europe, we also want to play harder and eat more, drink more and lead a more lavish lifestyle than the rest of Europe. We buy land and property as if it was going out of fashion and we have embraced a consumer paradise. We spend, spend, spend on everything to such an extent that our personal debt now exceeds income at 130 percent. We have become a nation of property investors and speculators at home and abroad. We have created a huge wealthy, middle-class where expectations are high and aspirations and hopes are fuelled by a vibrant property market and economy.

vs

THE OLD 20th CENTURY IRELAND

Who We Were

Since Ireland received its freedom from England in 1922, our core values have centered around patriotism and nationalism, the Catholic Church and other icons of our Irishness such as the language, the GAA and our civil war political parties. We clung onto the past and spoke of 1916, the civil war and the famine. We had a huge inferiority complex and our expectations were based on survival and 'know your station'. We were a nation of under-achievers and begrudgery was part and parcel of our way of being. We were generally pessimistic, inward looking and took the view that today governs tomorrow. We accepted hardship as part and parcel of what we deserved. We were lost for most of the 20th century and made the miraculous transformation as the 21st century clocked in.

What We Did

The old Ireland operated on a survival instinct. We had a major inferiority complex for most of the 20th century. We accepted the inevitable, almost as a punishment that we deserved. Unemployment rates had hit almost 20 percent and were seen as the norm. Our brightest and best educated young people emigrated in their hundreds of thousands during the 1980s and early 90s. We defended our worst excesses with well-argued excuses and developed a national blame culture second to none. We wallowed in civil war politics and borrowed to the extent that in 1985 public borrowing was at 130 percent of income. For the last 30 years of the 20th century, 'the North' dominated every news bulletin and just added to the depression and recession ethos that pervaded the nation.

APPENDIX 2

FREQUENTLY ASKED QUESTIONS

After reading *Crossing the Rubicon* and before you embark on writing your personal strategy workbook you may have some clarification questions. Here are some of the most frequently asked questions about *crossing the rubicon*:

WHY DO WE NEED SEVEN STEPS?

Rubicon is an integrated, all embracing, process. The personal side seeks to answer the question *who I am* and the professional side seeks to answer the question *what I do*. This double process runs through the seven steps.

Further, there are four dimensions to the human being – physical, intellectual, emotional, spiritual – and rubicon endeavours to integrate all these elements into one whole, working on the principle that the whole is greater than the sum of its parts.

To grow and change and live a worthwhile and fulfilling life, you need to see everything in total context. Context is a mindset. It is the panoramic view. It is like trying to fit pieces of a jigsaw together without seeing the full picture first. When you see the picture you are trying to create, putting the individual pieces of the jigsaw together becomes relatively easier. Everything is relative. When asked to describe his theory of relativity, Albert Einstein said "When you sit with a nice girl for two hours, it seems like two minutes. When you sit on a hot stove for two minutes, it seems like two hours".

To combine the softer parts of strategy – values and mission – with the more operational planning aspects of strategy – goal setting and tactical plans – requires a master blueprint so that you can see the wood from the trees, and the parts from the whole. Goals are the more logical, left-brain, practical aspects of strategy, while mission and vision are the more intuitive and emotional strategy in action.

The whole purpose of rubicon is to help you see the big picture and get the right balance between the operational side of your life and the human/emotional side of your life. For many people this is called work/life balance. For me, it is like walking a tightrope where the constant challenge is to stay balanced as we journey through life.

WHAT'S WRONG WITH JUST HAVING GOALS?

Goals on their own can just confuse people and leave them feeling empty. Interestingly, the origin of the word 'goal' comes from the old English word 'gol' which means to hinder or overcome an obstacle. Goals-driven people often feel deflated because of the huge effort to overcome the barriers or roadblocks that achieving goals needs. In fact, achieving goals without the proper clarity and focus around your purpose and values can do more harm than good. Many executives, for example, achieve the goals they set with regard to climbing the corporate ladder only to realise the pointlessness of it all and that the ladder, in fact, was leaning against the wrong wall. Purpose breathes life into what you do. Purpose is about being. Goals are about doing.

People who concentrate on just goals frequently get goals handed to them by their boss or other people and frequently become task oriented and absorbed in To Do lists in the belief that the achievement of the goal is everything. Achievement of a goal is not everything. No matter how big that goal is, it must be part of a bigger context, a bigger purpose and consistent with your underlying thought process, values and character.

Some people are paralysed by the past, others are transfixed by the future. But there is an old saying that goes "If you keep one eye on the past and one eye on the future, you will become cross-eyed in the present". The lesson is to enjoy today, live in the present, work and live in context.

Too much of a good thing can destroy you. Too much of a focus on goal setting and achievement can destroy you. Just as a strength overused can become a weakness, so can the embrace of the goal setting tool on its own do you collateral damage.

So, goals are good, but in context. The end does not always justify the means. Consider the means. The seven steps of rubicon are means, not an end. Goals are one piece of the pie, not the total pie.

Rubicon, therefore, is beyond just goal setting. It is beyond just achieving things. It is beyond the job or financial benchmarks that so many people consciously or unconsciously seek to reach in their own journey.

IT'S JUST TOO MUCH, TOO ALL EMBRACING, I'LL NEVER GET AROUND TO IT. WHAT SHOULD I DO?

Context again. If you are a man, your life expectancy is 75.1 years. That is 657,876 hours. If you are a woman, your life expectancy is 80.3 years. That is 703,428 hours. Planning and organising your life surely must be worth 100 hours.

The biggest challenge with rubicon, like all the great challenges in life, is simply getting started. But remember, any system is better than no system, and rubicon provides you with a ready made blueprint that thousands of people have already soldiered through, and ironed out the glitches to ensure that your crossing will be so much easier.

Everyone has their own preferred way to learn, some people just like to jump in and start, while others like to reflect and consider before taking the first step. Both ways have merit and both ways work.

WHAT ABOUT 'HORSES FOR COURSES'? IS THIS FOR EVERYONE?

Every activity in life can be seen as an experiment. There is a lot of truth in the old saying "When the student is ready the teacher will appear". Like everything in life, you may not be ready. You may need to experiment some more. This of course is your right. All truth is your truth. If you think this will not work for you right now, then you are probably right. Don't do it. Experiment some more. Maybe another time and place in your life would be more appropriate.

Rubicon is a systems thinking way of looking at the world. Galileo once said that you cannot teach an adult something they do not already know. Systems thinking merely allows you to get the edge you may be seeking or organise your thoughts, or understand the voices in your chatterbox, or create a master map that acts as a reference point at various times. But in the end, you decide. Context is everything.

Why Should I Do All This, Why Don't I Just Keep Going The Way I Am?

I remember taking a one-week presentation skills course in Vancouver, Canada, many years ago. First, we were taught the principles of good communication. Beginners learned how to make good eye contact and use their hands. As we progressed, we got more and more advanced and learned about facilitation and presentation techniques that professional speakers use, such as functional movement, right brain stories and positional power. We then learned about different techniques and which techniques are best used with different kinds of audience situations.

The lessons about principles continued for the first few classes, until we were ready to start making a live presentation to the class. At this stage, we were drilled into using the techniques that we had just learned. During technique training we were forced to use the exact technique as taught and incorporate it into our presentation to best effect. With the help of these techniques we were able to make great presentations with predictable and repeatable results.

This is why the best professional presenters and public speakers, after using systems and techniques during their training, progress from the safety of the methodology and revert back to fundamental principles. They begin to ad-lib on stage and play with their audience. They no longer rely on a specific formula. They 'free-wheel'. A good presenter becomes great primarily because they used the system and every best practice they could get their hands on in the beginning. To truly connect you need to go beyond the formula and try new things. *Crossing the rubicon* is a chance for you to pull everything together into one place in the first instance. Later, you can 'fly like an eagle' and improvise in your own way.

Goal setting and achieving on their own can become addictive and, in fact, a crutch that churn out predictable results. This can be very useful, as you can imagine, but it can also be very limiting. It reduces your ability to see the big picture and the overall context in which you play the game.

Why Does Rubicon Work?

It works for several reasons and at several levels. First, making a valuable contribution or living a worthwhile life is closer to your hand than you may think and by labouring through the exercises in the current situation analysis you, hopefully, come to realise that your current experiences, talents and passions are good enough to help you achieve whatever it is you want to achieve. Your current position is the launch pad. When you start to get a different appreciation of success and the talents and resources that are available to you, you start to make different choices about change and work/life balance.

Second, rubicon allows you to appreciate the now, at first hand, in the form of your fundamental beliefs, principles, values and purpose, and simultaneously, challenging you to write goals that are consistent and in harmony with these values. Success is not just achieving the goals you set. Success is embracing the twin aspects of *who you are* and *what you do*.

Third, ironically, when you have your rubicon document formulated, you can try less hard and this allows the intuitive elements of luck and opportunity to invade your life. Mental focus and clarity become less important because you have captured everything in written form. Therefore, you can apply clarity and focus to everyday occurances and allow amazing things to happen. Your head is clear to meet people, see solutions to problems and make connections between completely unrelated things.

Fourth, boldness and courage enter your life as never before, and you automatically become more adventurous and open to possibility, opportunity and fun that if you hadn't the big picture organised you would simply have no time to entertain.

Fifth, when you get your big thinking, emotional intelligence and operational affairs flying in formation, you start to attract people, circumstances and apparently lucky episodes into your life. Chance happenings suddenly make sense. Trying to prospect for customers is far less successful than the indirect effort of peer level networking.

APPENDIX 3

WORDS FROM THE WISE: THE CHALLENGES OF CROSSING THE RUBICON

"Nothing in this world can take the place of persistence. Talent will not; nothing is more common than unsuccessful people with talent. Genius will not; unrewarded genius is almost a proverb. Education will not; the world is full of educated derelicts. Persistence and determination alone are omnipotent." – Calvin Coolidge

"Our greatest glory is not in never falling, but in rising every time we fall."
– Confucius

"If you can force your heart and nerve and sinew to serve your needs long after they are gone, and so hold on when there is nothing in you except the Will which says to them: Hold on!" – Rudyard Kipling

"I know of no such unquestionable badge and mark of a sovereign mind as that of tenacity of purpose …" – Ralph Waldo Emerson

"Do what you can, with what you have, right where you are."
– Theodore Roosevelt

"Many men fail because they quit too soon. They lose faith when the signs are against them. They do not have the courage to hold on, to keep fighting in spite of that which seems insurmountable. If more of us would strike out and attempt the impossible, we very soon would find the truth of that old saying that nothing is impossible … abolish fear and you can accomplish anything you wish."
– Dr. C. E. Welch

"Men who have blazed new paths for civilization have always been precedent setters. It is ever the man who believes in his own ideas;

who can think and act without a crowd to back him; who is not afraid to stand alone; who is bold, original, resourceful; who has the courage to go where others have never been, to do what others have never done, that accomplishes things, that leaves his mark on his times. Don't wait for extraordinary opportunities, seize common ones and make them great." – Orison Swett Marden

"Nothing can resist the human will that will stake even its existence on its stated purpose. The secret to success is constancy of purpose." – Benjamin Disraeli

"I am not discouraged, because every wrong attempt discarded is another step forward." – Thomas Edison

"We will either find a way or make one." – Hannibal

"Life is either a daring adventure or nothing." – Helen Keller

"You must be courageous, and courage is the capacity to go from failure to failure without losing any enthusiasm." – Winston Churchill

"The credit belongs to the man who is actually in the arena; whose face is marred by sweat and blood; who strives valiantly; who errs and comes short again and again; who knows the great enthusiasms, the great devotion, and spends himself on a worthy cause; who at best knows in the end the triumph of high achievement; and who at the worst, if he fails, at least fails while daring greatly."
– Theodore Roosevelt

"Do not pray for tasks equal to your powers. Pray for powers equal to your task." – Phillips Brooks

"The problem with most failing businesses is not that their owners don't know enough about finance, marketing, management, and operations – they don't, but those things are easy enough to learn – but that they spend their time and energy defending what they think they know. My experience has shown me that the people who are exceptionally good in business aren't so because of what they know, but because of their insatiable need to know more." – Michael Gerber

APPENDIX 4: CARRY ON

It's easy to fight when everything's right,
And you're mad with the thrill and the glory;
It's easy to cheer when victory's near,
And wallow in fields that are gory.
It's a different song when everything's wrong,
When you're feeling infernally mortal;
When it's ten against one, and hope there is none,
Buck up, little soldier, and chortle:
Carry on! Carry on!
There isn't much punch in your blow.
You're glaring and staring and hitting out blind;
You're muddy and bloody, but never you mind.
Carry on! Carry on!
You haven't the ghost of a show.
It's looking like death, but while you've a breath,
Carry on, my son! Carry on!

And so in the strife of the battle of life
It's easy to fight when you're winning;
It's easy to slave, and starve and be brave,
When the dawn of success is beginning.
But the man who can meet despair and defeat
With a cheer, there's the man of God's choosing;
The man who can fight to Heaven's own height
Is the man who can fight when he's losing.
Carry on! Carry on!
Things never were looming so black.
But show that you haven't a cowardly streak,
And though you're unlucky you never are weak.
Carry on! Carry on!
Brace up for another attack.
It's looking like hell, but you never can tell:
Carry on, old man! Carry on!

There are some who drift out in the deserts of doubt,
And some who in brutishness wallow;
There are others, I know, who in piety go
Because of a Heaven to follow.
But to labour with zest, and to give of your best,
For the sweetness and joy of the giving;
To help folks along with a hand and a song;
Why, there's the real sunshine of living.
Carry on! Carry on!
Fight the good fight and true;
Believe in your mission, greet life with a cheer;
There's big work to do, and that's why you are here.
Carry on! Carry on!
Let the world be the better for you;
And at last when you die, let this be your cry:
Carry on, my soul! Carry on!

– Robert W. Service

APPENDIX 5:

PROMISE YOURSELF

To be so strong that nothing can disturb your peace of mind.

To talk health, happiness and prosperity to every person you meet.

To make all your friends feel that there is something in them.

To look at the sunny side of everything and make your optimism come true.

To think only of the best, to work only for the best, and to expect only the best.

To be just as enthusiastic about the success of others as you are about your own.

To forget the mistakes of the past and press on to the greater achievements of the future.

To wear a cheerful countenance at all times and give every living creature you meet a smile.

To give so much time to the improvement of yourself that you have no time to criticise others.

To be too large for worry, too noble for anger, too strong for fear; and too happy to permit the presence of trouble.

To think well of yourself and to proclaim this fact to the world, not in loud words but in great deeds.

To live in the faith that the whole world is on your side so long as you are true to the best that is in you.

– **Optimist Creed by Christian D. Larson, 1912**

APPENDIX 6

ABOUT CENTURY MANAGEMENT

A strategy management consultancy established in 1989, in Ireland, Century Management is primarily engaged in strategic human performance improvement, culminating in organisation-wide systemic and cultural change, augmented by tailored learning and development programmes.

The Century Management mission is "To partner with our clients to create business advantage by *energising* individuals, teams and organisations to maximise their full potential."

Century Management are specialists in organisation change management, cultural transformation, strategic thinking and planning, and benchmarking leadership competencies through a strategic human performance improvement process.

The company has a core competency in the area of change management, especially in the areas of cultural transformation, internal communications, boardroom effectiveness, teambuilding, sales & marketing, leadership facilitation and executive coaching.

The core values of Century Management are:

- To conduct our business with energy, integrity and professionalism in a client focused team culture
- To continually improve the effectiveness of our solutions, services and products for the benefit and success of our clients
- To continuously learn and innovate in our personal, interpersonal, team, organisational and client developments
- To establish and develop mutually rewarding relationships with all our stakeholders.

The company frequently act as recruitment advisors, facilitate think-tanks with senior groups, conduct executive coaching and mentoring, conduct public speaking engagements and advise on succession planning, branding, marketing and exit strategy planning.

APPENDIX 7

ABOUT JOHN BUTLER

John Butler has more than 25 years experience in leadership development, sales and marketing management, managing change processes and strategic organisational development. He is a highly respected speaker, author and business advisor in many parts of the world.

Professional Speaker

John Butler is a professional speaker who provides the valuable lessons from more than 25 years of leadership and business building experience to each of his speaking and consulting assignments. As a speaker he can tailor an after-dinner talk, conference, seminar, special event or motivational speech to your requirements in strategic planning, sales effectiveness, management, communication skills, personal potential, employee and customer relations, team building and personal development. (for a list of topics and presentations he has conducted visit www.centurymanagement.ie/speaker). His talks and seminars have given thousands of business people around the world the key to survival, profitability and growth. He has conducted speaking engagements for clients in Australia, Canada, France, Germany, Sweden, Switzerland, South Africa, Turkey, USA, United Kingdom and in his home country of Ireland.

Successful Author

John Butler has written several successful business development programmes and books including: The Business Management Consultancy Programme, The Competency Programme, Outstanding Customer Care, Managing Outstanding Customer Service, Professional Presentation Skills, Face-to-Face Communications and Relationship Selling Excellence. He writes frequently for business magazines on various management and business related topics. His book ***Successful Entrepreneurial Management: How to Create Personal and Business Advantage*** has been described as 'the new synergy' for 21st century management and business success, which has been translated into the German language and sold widely in Germany. His book ***Know Yourself, Know Your Customer*** is co-authored with Frank Scheelen, published in

Hungary and Germany, and gives you an underlying insight into how people 'naturally' think, feel and act and how to connect with more and more people to achieve a win/win result. ***Odyssey: The Business of Consulting*** is a process where he consults with consultants around the world.

Business Advisor

John Butler wears several consulting hats, depending on the client situation, such as: advisor, action planner, catalyst, challenger, change agent, coach, confronter, expert on-call, facilitator, listener, mediator, mentor, presenter, strategist, and supporter.

Careers in management, marketing, publishing, education, sales, distribution, consulting and organisational development are the bedrock of the wealth of experience and knowledge that he brings to each consulting and organisational development engagement. He is a practitioner, constantly learning, improving and passing value to clients. His strategy sessions have prompted thousands of business leaders to rethink their real/best contributions to their organisations.

He is first and foremost, however, an entrepreneurial businessman and he is constantly applying these ideas and techniques within his own businesses, client organisations and consulting companies.

APPENDIX 8

ODYSSEY: THE BUSINESS OF CONSULTING

Running a successful, profitable, consulting business is one of the toughest challenges in business today! So what are the strategies and tactics to manage, grow or transform a consulting business?

Delivering a 'professional service' is unique and different to a normal business in many ways — therefore it needs special attention in terms of a business model, marketing management, implementing best practice consulting processes and constantly changing business applications.

Odyssey: The Business of Consulting is the result of a focus by John Butler, over a 10 year period, on how independent consulting practices and small consulting firms operate in many parts of the world. The primary focus is on marketing, selling, positioning and building a profitable consulting business.

Odyssey is a journey to becoming a leading edge practitioner as a professional consultant. It teaches consultants how to transfer best practice theory relevant to client needs whilst empowering them to solve their own problems.

By completing the ODYSSEY consultants will:

- Clarify critical success factors to transform their consulting business

- Understand the five 'purpose areas' of management consulting and 10 ways consultants 'intervene'

- Understand the self-image consultant irony and how to master it

- Appreciate, more fully, the nature, ethics, roles and expectations of consulting

- Create THE most essential prerequisite with the client

- Have the mindset shift from traditional consulting to results-based consulting

- Recognise the power of four critical leverage points

- Execute three essentials that consultants advise on, but 'forget' to apply to themselves.

John Butler works with consultants from all over the globe over a six month period on practical client assignments and integrating best practice principles into their consulting business.

Where to buy the Workbook or eWorkbook

Writing Your Personal Strategy

Formulating The Seven Strategy Steps From The *Rubicon* Model

The primary objective of *"Writing Your Personal Strategy"* workbook is to bring clarity and focus to *who you are* and *what you do* IN A WRITTEN FORMAT.

You may choose to hand-write in this workbook, or use it as part of your start off thinking process before typing the final copy into the electronic version. There is something very powerful, however, about the touch and feel of the hand-written approach. The electronic version is of course tighter and neater. Why not work both methods? Personal choice prevails!

This workbook is best completed by following a parallel process with ***Crossing the Rubicon*** which outlines the seven step master formulation in great detail. Cross referencing from one to the other is the idea. The workbook has lots of templates and fill-in spaces to allow you to 'stamp your own thumb-print' on it.

When you have fully completed the workbook – handwritten or electronic – you will have your own written book. Like most things in life the first time you complete this exercise will be the most time consuming. The updates and additions over the years become relatively simple.

You will be amazed how you have grown and changed over a couple of years even.

Writing your personal strategy is a forced response exercise. It puts you on the spot to answer top of mind questions and in most cases what you write will be very accurate in your first attempt. Be sure to keep copies of your original and second edits. This can bring a smile to your face when you see how you were thinking five or 10 years ago.

'Writing Your Personal Strategy' workbook (120 pages) is available in CD or paper version at €15.00 each or €20.00 for both.

Email: info@centurymanagement.ie or telephone: 00 353 1 4595950.

INDEX

A

Achievement Orientation, 106
Achilles Heel, 157
Alameda Study, 29
Alexander the Great, 154
American Railways, 40
Appreciation, 32
Ashe, Liz, 152
Australia, 93, 113, 180
Authority Conflict, 106

B

Baez, Joan, 112
Bailey, Pearl, 56
Balance, 21
Balance Sheet, 26
Battle of Egypt, 164
Battle of Waterloo, 156
Benchmarking, 51, 85, 179
Best Practice, 13, 33, 134, 139, 144, 182
Bible, 40, 122
Body Mass Index, 30
Boldness, 19
Boucicault, Dion, 53
Brainstorm, 114
Buffet, Warren, 63
Burke, Edmund, 113
Business Advisor, 181
Business of Consulting, 181
Business Owners, 63
Butler, John, I, 12, 166, 180, 181, 182, 183

C

Caesar, Julius, 13
Career Assessment, 104
Career Diversification, 93
Career Planning, 17, 183
Casson, Herbert, 118
Celtic Tiger, 46, 61
Central Bank in Ireland, 71
Century Management, 1, 41, 179
Change, 81
Childhood Obesity, 30
Choke Point, 44, 49, 52, 54, 55, 98
Churchill, Winston, 19, 164, 176
Coca Cola, 41
Commitment, 20, 23, 79, 147, 159
Communication, 32
Competencies, 33
Competition Authority, 64
Confucius, 13, 175
Continuous Improvement, 83
Core Values, 112, 113, 114, 115, 142, 179
Corporate Managers, 64
Creating Business Advantage, 41
Creative Class, 64
Creativity and Innovation, 97
Critical Success Factors, 40, 66, 86, 98, 129, 130, 138, 182
Crossing the Rubicon, 3, 12, 13, 19, 58, 73, 74, 77, 100, 105, 134, 164, 166, 175, 183
Current Situation Analysis, 24, 26, 100
Current Status, 38

D

Danish Cartoonists, 113
Danko, William, 59
Darion, Joe, 125
Darius Of Persia, 154
D-Day, 162
Decisiveness, 127
Define the Job, 86
Desert Storm, 158
Develop and Implement Appropriate Solutions, 86
Discipline, 127
Dobson, Henry Austin, 52
Domino's Pizza, 162
Dreams, 123, 125
Drucker, 94, 152, 160, 161

E

Early Influences, 103
Effective, 75
Efficient, 75
Eight Strategy Ingredients, 183
Einstein, 31, 69
Eisenhower, 148
Elizabeth I, 52
Emerging Priorities, 100
Emotional Maturity, 105
Entrepreneurs, 66, 72, 94
Eu-Stress, 108

Index

F

Family Life, 103
Fear, 20, 22, 28, 69, 126
Federal Express, 41
Financial Freedom, 34
Financial Literacy, 68, 69, 130
First Nature, 88
Fishing Pool, 103
Five Drivers to Creating Wealth, 65
Foch, F., 152
Focus, 23
Forced Reponse, 24
Forster, E. M., 31
Four Change Options, 81
Four Colours, 87
France, Anatole, 56
Freud, Sigmund, 71
Frugal, 59
Fundamental Strategy Principles, 145, 146

G

Gandhi, Mahatma, 81, 113, 137
Gates, Bill, 63, 148, 154, 165
Gaugamela, 154
Gerstner, Lou, 160
Glasson, George, 156
Goal Setting, 17, 75, 106, 134, 135, 136, 139, 144, 183
Goethe, 37
Good Physical Health, 29

H

Hamlet, 39
Happiness, 27
Hardiness Test, 107
Health, 104
Hewlett, Bill, 14
High Net Worth Individuals, 61
Hill, Napoleon, 127, 152
Hobbies, 104
Home and Work Life, 21
Hubbard, Elbert, 122
Hummel, Charles, 137
Hussein, Saddam, 158

I

IBM, 41, 154, 160
Identity Management, 51
Important Tasks, 76
Inborn Leadership, 34
Income Generation, 56
Ingredients of Success, 13, 27, 35
Intangible Assets, 52
Intangible Resource, 49
Intellectual Capital, 50
Internal Motivator, 88
Invasion of Russia, 158
Irish Salary Surge, 62
Israeli-Arab 1967 Six-Day War, 162

J

Jefferson, Thomas, 112
Job Experts, 86
Job Security, 33
Jung, Carl, 87

K

Keats, John, 39
Kennedy, John F., 122
Key Accountabilities, 79, 86
Key Result Areas, 53, 74, 96
King, Martin Luther, 124
Kipling, 160
Knowledge Management, 50, 96

L

Labour Under Correct Knowledge, 57
Landor, Walter, 51
Levels of Wealth, 60
Life Expectancy Figures, 52
Locus of Control, 108
Long Term Perspective, 72
Luck, 57, 58, 135, 166
Luck Project, 57

M

Mackenzie, 148
Macleish, Archibald,, 119
Macro Change, 81, 84
Magnificent Obsession, 23, 33, 66, 122, 125
Mahan, 150
Manoeuvre, 15, 146
Market Development, 92
Marsten, William Moulton, 87
Maslow, Abraham, 37
Mass Affluent, 60
McWilliams, David, 46
Mental Stability, 107
Micro Change, 83
Microsoft, 41, 63
Mission, 24, 118

Index

Mission Statement, 118
Moment of Insight, 40, 100
Moments of Service, 128
Money Resource, 45
Murrow, Edward R., 109

N

Napoleon, 127, 150, 160
Natural Behaviours, 50, 85
Networking, 70, 144
Nike, 37
Normandy, 162
Northcote Parkinson, C., 53

O

OOMMEEES, 146, 147, 149, 151, 153, 155, 157, 159, 161
Outstanding Customer Care,, 180

P

Packard, David, 14
Pareto Principle, 74
Parkinson, 53
Parkinson, C. Northcote, 156
Parkinson's Law, 53
Passion and Focus, 66
Passive Income, 68
Pasteur, Louis, 58, 152
Pathways To Becoming Wealthy, 63
Patrick Kavanagh,, 74
Patton, 150, 154, 156, 162
Patton, George, 143
Pearl Harbour, 162
People Resource, 54
Personal Coaching, 17, 183
Personal Development, 84
Personal Identity and Image, 97
Personal Market Penetration, 92
Personal Strategy, 12, 13, 15, 17, 18, 19, 20, 22, 29, 40, 44, 45, 46, 48, 50, 73, 74, 75, 77, 78, 91, 92, 95, 100, 102, 105, 112, 131, 136, 146, 164, 166
Personal Strategy Workbook, 114
Personal Transformation, 85, 94, 105
Personal Values, 108
Pew Survey, 113
Physical Resource, 47
Pleasure Principle, 70
Pope John Paul Ii, 123
Popes Children, 46
Positioning, 16, 47
Poverty Consciousness, 68
Presentation Skills, 180

Principle of Economy, 146
Principle of Execution, 146
Principle of Exploitation, 146
Principle of Manoeuvre, 146
Principle of Mass, 146
Principle of Objective, 146
Principle of Offensive, 146
Principle of Surprise, 146
Proactive, 74, 75, 77, 78, 79, 143
Procedural Change, 83
Procrastinating, 70
Product Resource, 46
Product/Market Growth Matrix, 91
Professional Development, 94
Professionals, 64
Promise Yourself, 178
Psychology of Time Management, 165
Psychosomatic Symptoms, 108
Purpose, 19, 171
Purposeful Work, 32
Pyrrhic, 156

Q

Quality Relationships, 31

R

Ralph Waldo Emerson, 37, 175
Reactive, 74
Reade, Charles, 112
Reading, 39, 93
Realism, 18
Relationship Selling Excellence, 180
Resources Analysis, 43
Respect, 31
Responsibility, 19, 125
Reviewing Your History, 24, 102
Roman Empire, 113
Routine Change, 83
Rubicon River, 13, 17

S

School Years, 103
Schwarzkopf, 148
Self Actualisation, 35
Self-Image, 107
Setting Priorities, 165
Shakespeare, 21, 37, 39, 53, 108
Shenstone, William, 39
Skills Inventory, 96
Smart, 123, 134, 139, 142, 144
Social Life, 104
Socrates, 84
Stanley and Danko, 156

Stanley, Thomas, 59
Stewart, Thomas A, 50
Strategia, 16
Strategic Goals, 24, 134
Strategic Human Performance Improvement, 86
Strategic Planning, 14, 15, 163
Strategic Thinking, 14, 17, 163
Strategy Execution, 100, 136, 163, 165
Strategy Formulation, 12, 24, 26, 112, 134, 136, 163
Success, 27
Successful Entrepreneurial Management, 12, 180
Successful Entrepreneurs, 66
Sun Tzu, 148
Switzerland, 113, 180
Swot Analysis, 95

T

Tactical Planning, 24, 142
Tactical Plans, 142
Talent Analysis, 85
Talents, 22, 26, 85, 96, 125, 135
The Business of Consulting, 182
The Millionaire Next Door, 59, 71
The Paradox of Time, 52
Thinking, 39, 50, 96, 174
Thomas Edison, 37, 39, 176
Time, 52, 74
Time Resource, 52
Toffler, 148
Transformational Change, 81
Trust, 29, 31, 123
Twain, Mark, 150

U

Ultra Wealthy, 62

Urgent Tasks, 76
Utilitarian, 89

V

Values, 22, 108, 112, 114, 116, 136
Values, 24, 112
Van Dyke, Henry, 78
Village Blacksmith, 71
Vision, 24, 122, 130, 131, 138
Vision Statement, 128, 129
Visionaries, 124, 125, 126
Von Clausewitz, Karl, 148

W

Weak Link, 43, 44, 52
Webster's Dictionary, 59
Wellington, 156
What Is Personal Strategy, 17
What Is Strategy, 14
What You Do, 21, 27, 33, 36, 38, 49, 51, 71, 73, 75, 88, 102, 105, 107, 112, 114, 118, 123, 183
Who You Are, 21, 27, 29, 33, 36, 38, 51, 71, 105, 107, 112, 118, 123, 183
Why Write a Personal Strategy, 20
Winning Edge, 55, 124
Winston, Thomas, 127
Workbook, 12, 22, 24, 29, 95, 100, 105, 115, 131, 164, 166
World Health Organisation, 18, 30, 45
World War II, 143
Writing, 15, 17, 20, 24, 37, 38, 39, 96, 105, 118, 120, 136, 170
Writing Your Personal Strategy, 12, 22, 24, 164, 166
WWII, 158

ISBN 141209535-2